UNDERSTANDING
PEOPLE

CHILDREN

YOUTH

ADULTS

by
Robert Barron, M.A.
J. Omar Brubaker, M.A.
Robert E. Clark, Ed. D.

Christian Education Faculty
Moody Bible Institute

EVANGELICAL TRAINING ASSOCIATION
110 Bridge Street, Box 327
Wheaton, Illinois 60189-0327

Third Edition
6 5 4 3
8 7 6 5 4 3 2

Library of Congress Catalog Card Number: 75-172116
ISBN: 0-910566-15-1

Contents

INTRODUCTION

Have you ever stopped at a high mountain overlook and looked down on the road you have just traveled? You knew what each traveler could expect and what experiences the drivers already had. You were in an advantageous place to understand both the problems and successes of driving on that road.

Understanding People is a mountaintop book. It places you in an advantageous position to view human development so you can more readily understand normal progress people make on the highway of life. Grasping its content will help you better relate to people. This knowledge will also help people with family relationships as well as sharing the truths of God with others.

The book opens with a brief introduction to human development from a Christian perspective. Later chapters take one age level and describe people at that age in terms of their physical, intellectual, emotional, social, and spiritual characteristics. Each chapter presents the theories of human development in an easy-to-read format with up-to-date practical applications of each theory.

You will notice each chapter concludes with discussion questions and activities to help you apply the contents. To help you focus your reading of the chapter, begin by reading these questions and activity descriptions. Then, when you finish your reading, take a few extra minutes and write your answers to these questions.

For those of you who desire more in-depth study of human development, at the end of the book you will also notice a list of resources for enrichment. Reading and studying a sampling of these resources will provide a more comprehensive study.

UNDERSTANDING HUMAN DEVELOPMENT

1

Is love God's greatest gift? Many people think so. Love, however, is not possible without the gift of life.

Importance of Life

To live life to the fullest, there must be recognition of the vast difference between making a living and building a life. Understanding the importance of life begins with realizing its great value.

Definition of Life

What is life? Life is something that is living. It is a quality that people, animals, and plants have and that rocks, dirt, and metals lack. Life also refers to the existence of an individual within certain time limits. These limits vary according to God's plan for each person (Ps. 31:15). When life is present, growth and reproduction are possible (World Book Dictionary).

A distinction must also be made between physical and spiritual life. Physical life begins at conception and ends at death. Humans, however, also are spiritual beings and can possess everlasting life which is forever. This word does not apply to anything else in the visible universe, including the sun and planets. Only humans are destined to live on after the suns of the universe have quenched their light.

Eternal life is a gift from God when a person receives Christ as Savior from sin and lasts throughout eternity. After believers' lives on earth are ended, they will be in heaven with Jesus if they know Him as Savior (Rom. 6:23; John 1:12; 3:36).

Value of Life

The value of life can be seen both in how people and God evaluate life.

Human Evaluation

Wars, religious beliefs, motivations, superstitions, and ideologies reveal much of how people value life. The differences in evaluation are easily seen by comparing the values in those nations which have retained some allegiance to Christian ideals to those which have rejected them.

In countries where Christian principles are practiced, a higher value is evidenced. Yet, the recklessness with which firearms are handled, drugs are used, abortions are performed, and automobiles are operated indicates life is little valued by many even in these areas.

God's Evaluation

After God judged the world by sending the flood, He committed the judicial functions of government into human hands. His instruction in Genesis 9:6, "Whoever sheds the blood of man, by man shall his blood be shed," shows how God values life. Life cannot be balanced by stocks or bonds, lands or gold. Only another life is of equal worth.

Christ said, "For what doth it profit a man, to gain the whole world and forfeit his life?" (Mark 8:36 ASV). God computes the value of life in the highest of all known terms.

Major Divisions in Life

There are three major divisions, or periods, in life: childhood (birth-11 years), adolescence (age 12-17, though some researchers may include later adolescence from ages 18-24 as part of the adolescent period), adulthood (18 and up). Each division has its distinctive characteristics and needs.

Childhood (birth-11 years)

Children are not miniature adults. They are persons living in a period of dependence and preparation. Childhood lays the foundation for the remaining years of life. Part of this period includes the vital preschool years in which children are developing their personality structures and forming lifelong habits.

Childhood is important. Christ became a child and used children to illustrate spiritual truths such as true simplicity, humility, faith, and trust (Matt. 18:2-6). Christ intervened when His disciples refused children permission to come to Him and He welcomed them. Then He urged them, "See that you do not look down on one of these little ones. . ." (Matt. 18:10).

Adolescence (12-17)

Adolescence, the second major division, means "to grow up" and includes the teenage years. Sometimes college or career years also are included. Young people seek their independence during this period and begin to understand themselves as total persons. Great changes take place physically and they reach new intellectual heights. Their emotions are in flux and they pursue reality in the Christian experience. They often doubt counsel from teachers or parents and want to make decisions for themselves.

The period serves as transition from childhood to adulthood. Adolescents begin to discover what contributions they can make. As they struggle to find themselves, they are often misunderstood. With careful guidance and direction, however, they can emerge with a well-balanced personality.

Adulthood (18 and up)

Various events are associated with becoming an adult. Voting age, military service, college and career pursuits, marital status, and the amount of responsibility people assume all affect movement into adulthood.

Adulthood is a continuing process of growth and maturation. Adults are usually classified as young, middle, or senior adults, using age as the guideline. While adulthood involves some degree of stability, adults live a complex life. They may, however, slip into a rut in daily life patterns and find it difficult to accept new challenges. Maturity depends upon total lifestyle and the ability to cope with problems and decisions.

Growth and Development Theories

It is possible to recognize patterns and stages in human growth and development. These development patterns help clarify needs and aid leaders to serve people. Many researchers have contributed to our understanding of human development. The most recognized theories are presented here.

Basic Needs

A need may be defined as "a lack of a necessary element in life, a requirement which must be met." Food, water, and shelter are basic needs that everyone has. These must be met in order to survive. As these needs are met, others rise in importance. Then, psychological needs such as affection, acceptance, security, power, and achievement supersede physical needs.

Maslow describes basic needs as being organized within persons according to their level of importance to the individual. The diagram below identifies this progression:

When people's needs are not met, their total personality may suffer. Needs may be satisfied in a variety of ways depending upon the person's background, environment, and the extent of need.

Stages in Life

Each individual advances through various stages in life— all distinctly different— to maturity. The infant stage differs greatly from the junior high, but both contribute to the total development in the life span of the individual. For each stage three basic questions must be addressed: What is the person like? What does he/she need? What must be accomplished during this stage to insure normal growth and development?

Intellectual Stages

Jean Piaget describes four stages in intellectual development through childhood and adolescence which are distinct and qualitatively different: birth to about 2 years, a period during which children learn through experiences using their senses and self-discovery through activity; from about 2 to 7 years, during which children judge things by their appearance and begin to use symbols through language they are acquiring; from about 7 to 11 years, during which children are more logical, learn to classify and put items in sequence, and communicate through concrete thinking; from about 12 years through adulthood, during which thinking becomes more theoretical and abstract.

Psychosocial Stages

Erik Erikson described eight stages of development which encompass all ages of human life. He views personality formation as a continuing process throughout childhood, adolescence, and adulthood. Four of his stages relate to children through 11 years of age. These stages are: trust vs. mistrust (birth to 1 year), autonomy vs. shame and doubt (1 to 3 years), initiative vs. inferiority (4 to 5 years) and industry vs. inferiority (6 to 11 years). [2]

In adolescence and adulthood, he suggests four stages: ego identity vs. ego diffusion, intimacy vs. isolation, generativity vs. self-absorption, integrity vs. despair.

Erikson indicates that individuals must make major adjustments to their social environment and self in each stage of life. As the stages in life are presented in the following chapters, each stage Erikson has suggested will be integrated appropriately. [3]

Moral Development Stages

Lawrence Kohlberg identifies six well-defined stages at three different levels through childhood and adolescence based on a sense of right and wrong. These stages represent growth of moral concepts or ways of judging, and not moral behavior. His stages are based on Piaget's stages of cognitive development. The three different levels are: Level 1, based on punishments and rewards; Level 2, based on social conformity; and

Level 3, based on moral principles. As individuals develop in their thinking processes, they can make moral judgments, and examples of kinds of behavior which are typical at each level are identified. [4]

Developmental Tasks

During each stage, individuals should make certain progress and adjustments which are typical of that stage in life and need to be completed successfully. Failure to progress according to the normal age group pattern will lead to what Havighurst describes as "unhappiness in the individual, disapproval by the society, and difficulty with later tasks." [5]

Among the developmental tasks: four- to five-year-old children learn to dress themselves; six- to eight-year-old children learn to read and write; adolescents develop realistic concepts of themselves; young adults often select life partners or choose careers. Completing these tasks at each level indicates the degrees of maturity persons have reached.

Personality Development

For the Christian there are two aspects of personality development. One relates to the natural human personality and the other is the Christian personality.

Human Personality

Personality, in the natural human sense, is a term describing the total of what people are physically, intellectually, socially, emotionally, and spiritually. It includes every aspect and area of life. From birth personality is influenced and molded by many forces. Heredity and environment being the major forces. Within the environment, a person is influenced mainly by family, school, church, peer group, and society.

Christian Personality

Christian education provides an additional perspective in the development of personality. The goal should be a wholesome and well-balanced personality which means spiritual balance as well as intellectual, emotional, social, and physical.

For a Christian personality there must be a definite conversion experience (John 3:3). The sinful nature with which people are born must be changed (Rom. 3:23; 6:12; 6:23). Christ alone can give new life for He died for sinful people upon the cross (Acts 4:12). Everyone who receives Christ as Savior is born again and is given new life (John 1:12; 3:36).

Even when natural human personality is well developed, new birth is necessary for a mature, well-balanced Christian personality (Eph. 4:11-16). Christ provides for a person's spiritual development through the power of the indwelling Holy Spirit (Gal. 5:22,23). Parents and Christian leaders share by their example of personal experience and thus help others know the joy of an integrated Christian personality.

Major Forces in Personality Development

Heredity and environment interact with each other in developing unique personalities. Maturity results from these complex forces operating over an extended period of time. It is impossible to determine exactly how much heredity or how much environment contributes since they cannot be understood apart from each other. Heredity gives an innate capacity and sets boundaries for potential development. Environment cultivates or hinders the development. The individual's emotional structure combines them into a unique personality.

Heredity (Genetics, Nature)

From conception the unborn are persons and begin to develop uniquely as individuals through the prenatal period and the remainder of their lives after they are born. Characteristics are inherited through the genes of parents. A child may inherit a strong body with great athletic potential but not inherit an athlete's ability. Ability to learn is inherited. Knowledge is not. Few characteristics, however, are constant from generation to generation.

Environment (Culture, Nurture)

Environment, like heredity, cannot be understood alone, but it is easier to study. Children have little control over their environment. It is controlled by parents and those with whom they live. Later in life environment is more self-determined. The most important environmental influences affecting children are the family, school, church, peer group, and society.

The *family* is the key environment for the most impressionable years. Children are influenced by the sentiments, opinions, and moral standards where they live. Imitation comes first and comprehension later. In the home children must find the love, understanding, and training they need.

At home, and especially from parents, children also get their first and most enduring ideas of God. What they later hear in church often is evaluated by what they see in their parents during childhood.

Parental modeling of the Christian lifestyle is important during these impressionable years. They will be constant teachers by precept and practice, and will undoubtedly have great influence in laying foundations for their children's total personality development. Parents should think of the home as the basic teaching agency and all other agencies should be considered supplementary to the home and its environment.

The *school* attempts to develop the mind and body and to put the individual in possession of the great cultural and scientific heritages of the human race. At school the child should learn to communicate better and thus improve in the art of human relations. If attending a Christian school, the child has the added dimension of a God-centered education which supports family spiritual instruction.

The *church* is concerned with the whole person, but concentrates on spiritual development. A total church program with various ministries can provide a strong thrust to meet spiritual needs. Those who work with people in various church ministries can have powerful influence in the development of Christian personalities. A balanced program will help individuals mature in Christ.

The *peer group* provides the physical and social environment. Its influences and contributions should not be minimized. Everyone depends at least in part on some outside group to satisfy their physical and social needs. The leader of the peer group often is a strong influence and may determine the moral code of its individual members. When daily companions also are church friends, Christian growth and witness are made easier.

Society has the broadest sphere of influence which affects the growth and development of the individual. Societal norms and practices are passed on through culture. The socialization of children and youth is a lifelong process and is influenced by many different socialization agents such as family members, peers, teachers, bosses, and the media. Socialization forces individuals to deal with new situations and adapt to major changes throughout life.

Elements of Personality Development

The development of a person involves the physical, intellectual, emotional, social, and spiritual being. All of society contributes to this development with the family, church, and school playing the most significant roles. What is involved in each area of development?

Physically

The physical body is that which we see. It is the house in which each unique individual personality lives. Society places great emphasis on having healthy bodies. Paul refers to the body as "the temple of the Holy Spirit" and admonishes Christians to "honor God with your body." (I Cor. 6:19,20).

Intellectually

The intellectual refers to the functioning of the brain, mind, the thinking and knowing part of us. Individuals are born with the capacity for knowledge and intellectual growth. From their earliest hours, infants begin to develop intellectually. They pass through intellectual stages in their thinking processes. Parents, leaders, and teachers need to understand how individuals think and learn and help them develop their intellectual knowledge, skills, and capacities. Intellectual stimulation is important in each stage of life.

Emotionally

Emotions relate to the affective part of us and involve the expression of our feelings, appreciations, and attitudes. The emotional development of the individual affects every area of personality development. Individuals need to learn to express themselves emotionally and how to control their emotions.

Socially

Social development involves our interpersonal relationships with others. Individuals need to feel accepted, to belong, and to enjoy the company of God's people. They need to know how to relate to others and to develop social skills to communicate more effectively. In the epistles many references are made regarding effective interpersonal relationships and communication which emphasize the spiritual aspect as well as the social (Eph. 4:31,32; Phil. 4:1-5; Col. 3:12-17).

Spiritually

For the Christian, the most important aspect of development is the spiritual. It involves our relationship with God—recognizing our spiritual need as sinners to be saved from our sins; receiving Christ as Savior, growing up in Christ and becoming more like Him; serving Him individually and collectively as members of the Body of Christ. Spiritual development is accomplished through commitment and dedication, dependence on God, confession of sin, obedience of the Word of God, and prayer. It is a lifetime process that will culminate when we see Christ (Rom. 3:23; John 1:12; II Peter 3:18; Eph. 4:13; I John 3:2).

Understanding Personality Development

There are many sources of information which are accessible for understanding and meeting needs in personality development.

Studying the Bible

The Bible is an excellent source for gaining insight into human behavior. The true nature and needs of mankind are clearly set forth in the life-related passages of the Old and New Testaments. The Bible is the authority—the textbook. When well-studied, it provides the basis for ministering to all age groups.

Observing People

Observation is one of the best ways to study people in total personality development at all stages of life. Individuals and groups can be observed naturally in a variety of settings. Quality observations can provide much helpful information in understanding others.

Remembering Past Experiences

Unfortunately people often forget their experiences. In fact, they probably would not recognize themselves if an exact production of them at earlier ages could be furnished. Carefully considering previous experiences and sincerely attempting to recall reactions at the time can help greatly in understanding others.

Reading Literature

Books geared to various age levels will give specific information about characteristics and needs of children, youth, and adults. To gain insight into their thoughts, vocabulary, attitudes, behavior, aspirations, and dreams, those ministering to people should read literature written for, as well as about, the age group with which they are involved.

Utilizing Scientific Findings

Reports of scientific studies concerning human development are available. Governments often provide helpful pamphlets concerning developmental stages. Numerous reliable publishing houses offer textbooks on child, adolescent, and adult development.

Those working with a particular age group can gather their own less scientific findings through questionnaires and interviews with a select group of people. Even informal conversations with individuals provide useful information for better understanding of others.

Implications for Ministry

God has given the family and church responsiblity in developing the person. Every stage requires special treatment and methods. While the church concentrates on spiritual development, it should not neglect the total personality. Its total program can help the individual gain perspective on the importance of life and relationships. The church's responsibility is to work with the marvelous gift of life!

The church should work with— not replace— the home in developing balanced Christian personalities. This includes the most important responsibility of leading members of a family to Christ as Savior. Individuals should be able to find friends at church so the influence of the peer group will benefit Christian growth. A church program should utilize the four major elements of personality development: knowledge, worship, fellowship, and expression. The church should provide a biblical foundation upon which its people can base their decisions for action. A church educational program should include training classes, resources through the church library, and experiences with various age groups. Parents can profit from these opportunities as they seek to develop the potential in the lives of their children and firmly establish their own lives.

Summary

Life is God's greatest gift. Physical life begins at conception and continues until death. Everlasting spiritual life is given to those who receive Christ as Savior. God computes the value of life in the highest of all known terms. Life has many possibilities, but the potential is dependent on what people do with what God has given.

Life is divided into three major divisions: childhood, adolescence, and adulthood. Each division contributes to the total growth and development of the individual.

Personality development involves the total being. Everyone who receives Christ as Savior becomes a Christian personality. These individuals have the privilege of developing their personalities in accord with biblical principles and the will of God with the ultimate goal of becoming more like Christ in every aspect of life. The major forces in personality development are heredity and environment.

It is necessary for the individual to develop in all areas of personality physically, intellectually, socially, emotionally, and spiritually in order to become a mature and balanced person. We can have a better understanding of others through observation and study.

Notes

1. A. H. Maslow, "A Theory of Human Motivation," *Psychological Review*, vol. 50, no. 4 (1943), pp. 372-82.
2. Grace Craig, *Human Development,* 5th ed. (Englewood Cliffs, NJ: Prentice-Hall, 1989), pp. 35-38.
3. Craig, pp. 41-43.
4. Craig, pp. 352-355.
5. R. J. Havighurst, *Human Development and Education* (New York: David McKay Co., 1953), p. 2.

Discussion Questions

1. What evidences show life is important?
2. Name the three major divisions of life and identify what contributions each division makes in the total lifespan?
3. Identify some basic needs of every individual and tell what relationship these basic needs have in developing the total personality?
4. Identify and explain the stages intellectually (Piaget), psychosocially (Erikson), and morally (Kohlberg) through which people go and tell why each is important?
5. What do developmental tasks indicate?
6. How is personality defined and how is Christian personality distinctive?
7. What two major forces affect personality development?
8. Identify and describe the environmental influences which affect human development.
9. Name the elements of personality development and describe how each area contributes to total personality development.
10. How can we have a better understanding of the development of personality?

Application Activities

1. Using a Bible concordance, trace the biblical use of the word "life." List separately the temporal and spiritual significance. List verses in which Christ expresses the importance of life.

2. Collect recent stories or newspaper and magazine articles that indicate people's estimate of human life in childhood, adolescence, or adulthood. Report and discuss your findings.
3. Choose one of the following theories in human development. Trace and relate the basic concepts given in the text to real life situations: basic needs (Maslow); intellectual development (Piaget); psychosocial stages (Erikson); moral development (Kohlberg); developmental tasks (Havighurst).
4. Develop an information sheet you could use in analyzing the total personality of an individual. Compare your ideas with other members of the class and make a composite of the information for everyone in the class to be able to use.
5. Analyze one person you know using the information sheet developed in #4. Compare your findings with another person who did a study on the same individual at the same age.
6. Identify at least two practical ways in which the family, school, church, peer group, and society can influence the development of a personality for good.

Bibliography

Crabb, Lawrence J., Jr. *Understanding People: Deep Longings for Relationship.* Grand Rapids: Zondervan Publishing, 1987.

Getz, Gene. *Measure of a Family.* Ventura, CA: Gospel Light/Regal Books, 1977.

Graendorf, Werner C. *Introduction to Biblical Christian Education.* Chicago: Moody Press, 1981.

LeBar, Lois. *Focus on People in Church Education.* Westwood, NJ: Fleming H. Revell, 1981.

FOUNDATION YEARS

INFANTS AND TODDLERS

Birth through 24 months

2

As people move from infancy toward maturity, they travel through developmental periods in which people have somewhat similar characteristics. These characteristics are more clearly seen in a larger group but provide a basis for understanding individuals as well.

Acknowledging these similarities, those who study human development, both Christian and secular, regularly organize people into groups, enabling them to describe and study those of similar age characteristics.

The following divisions are widely used, although they may vary to allow people to have relationships that are alike in their church programs and ministries.

AGE	CLASSIFICATION
Birth-24 mos.	Infancy and Toddler
2 and 3	Preschool
4 and 5	Early Childhood
6, 7, 8	Middle Childhood
9, 10, 11	Later Childhood
12 and 13	Early Adolescence
14, 15, 16, 17	Middle Adolescence
18-24	Beginning Adulthood
25-34	Young Adulthood
35-64	Middle Adulthood
65 and up	Later Adulthood

Infants and Toddlers — *Foundation for the Future*

Subsequent physical, intellectual, emotional, social, and spiritual structure is built upon the foundation of early childhood. If the foundation is not properly laid in these most impressionable years, the entire superstructure strains.

The potential in every newborn child is tremendous. It is important that a child's first impressions be right impressions. Many of the perplexing problems faced later in life might be avoided by reaching children with the gospel— early! The church and the parent need to start working together at the very beginning— during infancy. A look at how infants and toddlers develop provides guidelines for ways to meet basic needs.

THE FIRST TWO YEARS

At birth . . . Normal babies usually exceed 6-1/2 pounds and are probably 20 inches long. They spend about 20 hours asleep each day.

One month . . . They have five to six daily feedings and sleep in two- to five-hour segments.

Six months . . . Their weight has doubled and they are five to six inches taller. They roll over easily and sit for short periods of time by themselves. Their vague sounds include cooing and gurgling.

Twelve months . . . They now are from 28 to 32 inches tall; their weight— usually 17-24 pounds. They might walk by now and use some two-syllable words. Parents can communicate effectively through simple vocabulary. They might have as many as six teeth or as few as two.

Eighteen months . . . They are a bundle of vigor all day long; measure between 30 and 33 inches; and weigh 21 to 27 pounds. They have 12 to 16 teeth.

Twenty-one months . . . Masters of walking and running, they are able to feed themselves quite well. All mental processes are developing rapidly. [1]

Physically — *Rapid Growers*

Infants grow rapidly in the first few months and progress steadily during their first year. They start out as tiny babies. Soon they are turning about and pulling themselves up in their cribs. Before long they are creeping and crawling. As their legs grow stronger they begin toddling from place to place. After that first step, they soon are walking almost everywhere. Developmental patterns vary greatly, but girls are usually ahead of boys in maturation.

Infants are continually active. They stretch, kick, wave their arms and legs, move their eyes, blink, cry, grasp. Through constant movement, children of this age grow and develop rapidly.

Activity Leads to Growth

The infant's chief business is growing. With a continuous round of eating, sleeping, and exercising, they will double their weight in the first six months. In their first year, their height increases fifty percent. Children naturally exert themselves in activities that promote growth.

Activity Leads to Development

Growth and development are not synonymous terms. Growth means to increase in size, function, and complexity up to maturity. Development implies change over time in structure, thought, and behavior caused by biological and environmental influences. The natural, God-intended development comes through physical activity. The body should also develop the senses and the intellect. Children gradually perceive and understand through impressions gained by touching, tasting, smelling, seeing, and hearing.

Intellectually — *Discoverers*

The deep longing to probe and discover is God-given and especially evident in infants and toddlers. By searching, man discovers the treasures of the universe. So the little child begins a long search for truth in both temporal and eternal matters.

Knowledge so familiar to adults is unknown to every child. This rapidly changes, however, for their activities help them discover and begin to understand. Even with their limited ability to express themselves verbally, it is amazing how much infants can comprehend in the early years.

Jean Piaget identifies the intellectual development of infants and toddlers as the period in which children use action schemes—looking, grasping, observing, tasting, touching—to learn about their world. The five senses are very sensitive to environmental influences and infants and toddlers respond to these different schemes. This development through actions and movements enable young children to explore and discover the world about them.

One of the first and greatest accomplishments during infancy is object permanence. Piaget indicates that when infants begin searching for things out of sight, they understand that objects continue to exist even if they cannot be seen. Thus, infants have taken a step toward somewhat more advanced thinking. They begin to use symbols to represent these things in their minds so they can think about them.

The second major accomplishment in this early period is when the child develops logical, goal-directed actions. Through trial and error the child learns how to manipulate materials to develop more difficult tasks which Piaget refers to as higher-level schemes. [2]

Emotionally — *Sensitive*

Infants and toddlers are very sensitive to surroundings and atmosphere. They may be afraid of strangers, unfamiliar situations, loud noises, or confusion. If children are frightened, they will retreat to their parent's or caregiver's arms. From about seven to nine months, children may go through what psychologists refer to as stranger anxiety. They may not want to leave their parents and go to unfamiliar people or situations. Adjusting to new environments or experiences may take several days or weeks and can be best accomplished through tender loving care expressed by parents and caregivers.

Sometimes when young children do not get their own way, they may express their displeasure through temper tantrums. Their emotions are intense. They may be laughing one minute and crying the next. Although their emotions are unstable, they begin to learn that certain types of behavior are acceptable or unacceptable.

Socially — *Limited to Immediate Surroundings*
Infants and toddlers live in a small world and interpret life through a limited self-centered viewpoint with themselves being the center of their world. As a result, they like the familiar and enjoy the immediate surroundings and members of their family. They learn quickly how to gain attention through sounds, gestures, and actions. They play individually but enjoy being entertained by others. Since these children are unable to communicate their needs, they depend almost entirely upon their family members and caregivers.

Erik Erikson describes the first stage in the child's social development as trust versus mistrust. Even before they are six months old, infants develop a sense of trust in people. This is particularly true in their relationships with their parents or other caregivers. Bonding is significant in building a trust relationship in the first few days and weeks of a child's life. Trust will enable these children to feel more secure with those who care for them as they adjust to new situations and experiences. If children do not learn to trust in infancy, they may have difficulty trusting others in later stages of development. [3]

Spiritually — *Dependent Upon Parents*
Young children acquire their patterns of conduct mostly through imitation. Actions of others have spiritual implications. Though these children do not understand the significance of the action, they imitate what they see and learn to pattern their lives for good or for evil. Young children's concepts of God are largely determined by their parents' concepts and attitudes toward Him.

Because their reasoning powers are very limited, infants are not capable of making moral judgments. They can begin to learn what is acceptable and unacceptable behavior, but most of their learning comes through imitation. Of course, even at this early stage of life, these children need positive models to follow in specific behaviors and attitudes.

The Home Prepares the Infant and Toddler
No individual can replace godly parents. God directed Pharaoh's daughter to the mother of Moses. All the wealth and wisdom of the

Egyptian court could not find a better teacher. Joseph and Daniel saw their parents' training sustain them amid the temptations of pagan pomp and power.

Very young children whose Christian parents willingly dedicate them to God have an early start toward spiritual success. When Christian leaders look back over their childhood, many come to realize that it was their parents' godly attitudes and dedication, along with the Holy Spirit's leading, that guided them to their ministries.

Implications for Ministry

The church ministers to infants and toddlers, from birth through 24 months, primarily through a church/home ministry.

This ministry might include: home visitation; a program during the Sunday school hour with activities for young children; Bible study and adult Sunday school classes for parents; a nursery during the worship services; and a periodic mothers' or parents' club meetings.

The church's ministry to infants and toddlers is a valuable asset in the spiritual development of little children. At an early age, these very young people can be ministered to by the church. This ministry serves at least three purposes:

To Welcome New Children

If little children are to be drawn to church relationship, more is needed than a simple church bulletin announcement of new babies' births or even sending greetings. Personal contact with the entire family and a definite effort to influence parents and siblings is necessary since these babies begin church identity through their families.

Parents should be encouraged to bring their babies to Sunday school and place them in the crib room and toddler classes while they attend an adult class and worship service. Babies thus experience the loving care of church workers and parents grow in spiritual understanding and ability to establish Christian homes. With such a program, the church will more adequately reach both its members and the community for Christ.

To Establish Contact Between Church and Home

Few homes are so indifferent to the claims of Christ that they object to the church welcoming their new babies into the Christian community. Even the most unchurched parents will happily remember a church staff member or volunteer visiting them in their home, expressing interest in their new baby, and welcoming the child into the church family. Besides opportunity for service, ministry to infants and toddlers tells the community the church is interested in families.

Even families who regularly attend church appreciate the attention shown to their new baby. New parents often need to be made aware of the ministries the church provides for them and their new son or daughter.

To Provide Parental Training

Since infant and toddler ministry is primarily carried on through the child's parents, it needs to focus its emphasis in this area. Primarily, adult classes and Bible studies for parents should stress the importance of the parental role in dedicating this gift of God back to Him and bringing up this new baby in the nurture and admonition of the Lord. Adult electives might include a class that centers on parenting infants and toddlers.

If church ministry to infants and toddlers includes a home visit, the visitor might give parents suggestions for: ways of beginning prayer times with the child, Bible story books and other materials which can be read to the child, or other helpful instruction on establishing a Christian home. This is very important when one realizes how much the child learns even before formal church instruction.

If the church is sincere in establishing an effective ministry to infants and toddlers, several workers will be needed: a director, home visitors, and workers for Sunday activities, including a trained nurse, if possible.

Those providing care and instruction to infants and toddlers should genuinely enjoy and be interested in young children. They must be gracious, friendly, pleasant, neat, and tactful and have an understanding of infants' and toddlers' characteristics and of the potential ministry to this age level. They should be ready to visit and able to keep confidences shared with them.

Summary

Infants and toddlers depend almost entirely on their parents and other interested persons for the development of personality. The church can also have an influence during this time through a structured program which includes parental instruction, adequate caring facilities, and educational programs for toddlers. The importance of the early years cannot be overemphasized.

Physically, infants and toddlers are growing rapidly. Intellectually, they are discovering the world about them. They are sensitive emotionally. Socially, they enjoy familiar surroundings and are dependent on parents for their spiritual development.

Infants and toddlers can be an important contact between church and home.

Notes

1. Margaret Jacobsen, *The Child in the Christian Home* (Wheaton, IL: Scripture Press, 1959), pp.21-35.
2. Robert Slavin, *Educational Psychology Theory Into Practice,* 2nd ed. (Englewood Cliffs, NJ: Prentice-Hall, 1988), p. 25.
3. Grace Craig, *Human Development,* 5th ed. (Englewood Cliffs, NJ: Prentice-Hall, 1989), p. 42.

Discussion Questions

1. Describe the total personality of infants and toddlers: physically, intellectually, emotionally, socially, and spiritually.
2. Why is activity important in the growth and development of infants and toddlers?
3. What responsibilities do parents have in preparing the child for life?
4. What are some of the values of church ministry to infants and toddlers?
5. What are the main purposes of the church's ministry to this age level?
6. What factors should be considered in establishing an effective church ministry to infants and toddlers?
7. How would you describe the ideal person to minister to infants and toddlers?

Application Activities

1. Interview the director of an infant and toddler ministry in a church to discover how the needs of the young child are met through this ministry.
2. Make a list of topics which can be developed in training classes for parents of infants and toddlers.
3. Role play a visit of a staff member, or visitation team, to the home of a prospective couple to welcome their infant into the church family and invite them to bring their family to church.

IMITATION AND DISCOVERY

PRESCHOOL

Ages 2 and 3

3

Ministering to twos and threes is more than babysitting. Children's educational television programs show that preschoolers can enjoy and benefit by programs emphasizing vocabulary building, number concepts, reading readiness, and concepts in socialization.

Until recently, the church was one of the few agencies providing preschool ministry. Through the years the church has been convinced that young children can learn basic spiritual concepts and develop right attitudes toward spiritual truths.

Preschool children are not simply getting ready for life. They are living it right now! For them the immediate present is more important than the future or the past. In these early years their personality structure is forming. Because attitudes are "caught as well as taught," they are more important to the preschooler than concepts or ideas.

The preschoolers' environment and associates will help or hinder the process of laying a good foundation for their lives. Parents have opportunity for the greatest influence on the life of the child since they are responsible for the child most of the day.

These children can learn simple concepts, attitudes, values, and behaviors basic to spiritual development. Bible teaching with much repetition of facts and concepts can be done to lay foundations for future learning and spiritual development. Both home and church must create an atmosphere of acceptance and of love as the small child develops.

Developmental Tasks
As the child progresses through preschool years, these achievements will indicate normal development:

Physical growth to three feet in height.
Ability to do some things for themselves.
Ability to communicate with simple vocabulary and sentences.
Awareness of others.
Grasp of simple spiritual concepts. [1]

Physically — *Active*

Preschool children engage in many kinds of physical and motor activities which are essential to normal growth and development. Because they are so active, they tire quickly and need balance between active and quiet activities.

Preschool children lack coordination in their larger muscles and have not developed their smaller muscles. They need to be able to move about freely. They cannot sit for long periods of time without moving. Therefore they must have activities to stretch growing bodies and to exercise muscles in acceptable forms of behavior. A large, spacious, carpeted room is ideal.

Are Susceptible to Disease

Preschool children are subject to common colds and illnesses. They lack physical strength to meet the demands of a full schedule, so regular attendance should not be expected or emphasized for two- and three-year-olds. A sick child in Sunday school or church endangers the health of other children. Plenty of fresh air and sunshine in a clean, cheerful atmosphere are necessary for active growing bodies.

Develop at Own Rate

Children develop at their own rates. They should not be compared with others in the group, especially those who are larger in size. Nor should more be expected from larger children. The program should be highly flexible permitting children to choose individual as well as group activities since they differ so widely in physical abilities.

Preschool children may have difficulty expressing themselves because of undeveloped vocal chords and limited vocabulary. Those working with twos and threes should not pressure them to sing on tune or urge them to sing loudly.

Intellectually — *Discoverers*

Preschool children discover their world through their senses. Color and texture, tone and volume, fragrance and flavor, warmth and coldness are sensations that provide learning experiences for them. They need to touch an object to get the "feel" of it through the senses.

These children sense and feel keenly many things that go unnoticed in adult life. Those ministering to preschoolers can capitalize upon the senses and provide opportunities for them to discover the world around them by direct experiences whenever possible.

Two- and three-year-olds are in transition from the stage of intellectual development whereby they learn through sensory experiences and activity to the stage during which they judge things by their appearance and begin to use symbols. This new stage begins about the time children are beginning to talk. They think in specifics rather than generalities and cannot think through the consequences of a particular chain of events. They judge things by the way they appear rather than on the basis of mental operations, and therefore, do not view things in proper perspective. They cannot tell the difference between the symbol and the object for which it stands. By the end of this period, these children learn that language is arbitrary and that one word can represent more than one object. [2]

Have Limited Attention Span

Most two- and three-year-olds will listen from two to five minutes depending on the level of personal involvement. When their maximum interest span has been reached, preschoolers will move on to another activity— planned or unplanned. Those working with this age level must be sensitive to this characteristic and adjust accordingly. All activities should be somewhat flexible but within limitations caused by group size. If these children want to return to an activity later, if possible they should be allowed to do so— with the spirit of discovery ever present.

Have Limited Vocabulary

The most common words in the preschooler's vocabulary are "no," "my," "me," and "mine." They learn new words and meanings from the older people in their lives.

The two- and three-year-olds may often say no although not always meaning it. At times they mean: "I can't do it," or "I don't understand what you want," or even, "Why?", or really, "No!" As they learn to express themselves verbally, they will grow out of this seeming negativeness. Some children tend to be more negative than others.

As new words are discovered, preschoolers are able to converse in simple language. Depending upon their exposure to records, tapes, books, and television, in their second year, preschoolers may have about 300 words in their active vocabularies— at three, about 900 words. Parents and others ministering to this age level should remember this before becoming impatient with the child. Baby talk should be avoided. Preschool children learn more through non-verbal communication— gestures, facial expressions, attitudes, emotional reactions— than they do through spoken words. In any teaching situation, children are learning much in addition to what is being presented.

Have Undependable Memory

Preschool children have short, undependable memories. Some things they may remember well, especially if the situation was traumatic; some things of lesser importance will be forgotten in a few moments. Twos and threes have great difficulty with recall and recognition since they are limited in their thinking processes. Visual memory seems to be strongest during this stage of life. Any activities which emphasize the five senses, familiar experiences, or personal involvement very likely will be remembered much better.

Have Limited Concept Understanding

Since preschoolers' concepts of time, space, and numbers are so limited, those ministering to this age level must speak in terms that they can grasp. "Long, long ago" and "far, far away" are much more appropriate and meaningful than "1000 years ago" or "2000 miles away." The world of preschool children is composed of present and familiar surroundings. Home is their main world. Often beyond that is unfamiliar territory. Parents and others working with preschoolers must learn to speak on their level with words that are specific, concrete, and literal. Words and concepts need to be repeated often and in a variety of ways and related to their everyday experiences.

Emotionally — *Fearful*

Twos and threes are emotionally unstable and express it by being fearful of the unfamiliar and by reacting to their surroundings.

Fear the Unfamiliar

Preschool children are fearful in crowds of people with the accompanying noise and confusion. They are familiar with their own home. In a new environment such as a Sunday school class, a day care center, or church, they may fear being left by their parents. Parents do not, however, need to remain with their children.

Those ministering to twos and threes can do much to help a child adjust smoothly to the new situation. If the church has a program of ministry to infants and toddlers, even newborns begin to recognize church workers and when brought to church and cared for in nursery facilities they continue to adjust to new faces and surroundings. Thus, as preschoolers progress into further class and ministry situations they often adjust more smoothly and are less frightened by new experiences.

Those who work with twos and threes should arrive early and be prepared and ready for whatever the situation. Then each child can be greeted personally upon entering the room and become involved in the planned activities.

Are Unstable Emotionally

One cannot be sure how the preschool child will react from one moment to the next. A child who begins to cry can be diverted by involvement in some activity. Fear will probably be the outstanding emotion, with most fears being learned from adults. Preschool children will imitate reactions they see as they encounter different situations.

React to Surroundings

Because of their active five senses, preschool children will react favorably or unfavorably to their surroundings. Rooms should be bright and colorful, warm and pleasant. The atmosphere should be one of efficiency with minimal confusion. Those working with this age level should model positive attitudes and actions as they relate to the children.

Socially — *Self-Centered*

The world of preschool children revolves around them, their home, and other familiar surroundings. In a wider world, they are still self-centered and fear the unfamiliar. The preschool child is a loner in play activities but enjoys parallel play alongside others.

Depend Upon Others

Erikson identifies the developmental stage for twos and threes as of autonomy versus doubt. Sometimes preschool children do not want to depend totally on others. They strive toward autonomy, or the ability to do things for themselves. Other times they become overdependent on adults and do not want to do things for themselves. They have the dual desire to "hold on" and "to let go." Parents and others ministering to this age level sometimes become frustrated trying to cope in meeting their needs.

There are times when children need assistance from adults. They need help getting dressed, tying their shoes, buttoning their coats, blowing their noses, and getting to church. Children need to explore freely and do things for themselves, but they also need an everpresent guiding hand to encourage autonomy. Wise parents and others working with this age level will allow children freedom within clearly defined boundaries. [3]

Prefer Playing Alone

Two- and three-year-olds often would rather play alone than with others. When with other children, they may appear to claim everything they see or touch and are not eager to share these things with others. Because of their limited attention span, they may drop what they momentarily claim and pick up something else which then becomes theirs.

Spiritually — *Imitators*

Preschool children imitate their parents and other adults who work with them as well as siblings. They may not understand the significance of certain actions but they imitate what they see and eventually pattern their lives after those they imitate. This often includes their feelings toward God.

No teaching is as powerful as the parents' quality of life. Children are quick to sense adult attitudes even before they understand the meaning of words. Christian parents teach when they lovingly care for their children, help one another, share with others, read the Word of God, and pray to their heavenly Father. All these actions show children how to live a godly life.

Wrong actions also are imitated early in life. Parents whose pressures, problems, and immature emotions are constantly reflected in their attitudes and actions will find their counterpart in restless and unhappy children.

Understand Basic Spiritual Concepts

Two- and three-year-old children are able to understand that the Bible is a special Book from God, Jesus is God's Son, the church is a place where they learn about God, and God loves and cares for them.

Preschoolers can understand that God loves them. They especially enjoy stories that relate to them and people their age like Jesus' birth and baby Moses. They can understand that Jesus grew up, and that He is their friend. As they begin to talk, they can learn to talk with God, but often become restless when adults require them to sit still during long prayers.

They can understand that the church is God's house and that in God's house they hear stories about Jesus and that there they see other children that Jesus also loves.

They can understand that the Bible is a very special book because it is God's Book, but cannot hold high respect for the Bible if adults leave it on a table or shelf, never read from it, or do not handle it carefully. Neither do they learn to appreciate it if adults only talk about it and never show them one.

Because of their undependable memory and limited vocabulary, concepts must be repeated over and over in a variety of ways. Preschool children enjoy this repetition.

Young children are not able to evaluate the consequences of right or wrong. They cannot distinguish between right or wrong and fact or fancy without help. Bible stories should always be labeled as true and taught from an open Bible.

Respond to Love

Emotionally and spiritually, preschool children want to be loved. They may seek attention in order to have this basic need met. Parents and other adults who work with this age level should emphasize the love of God for each child. Their understanding, care, friendliness, and love set the pace for happy relationships and effective learning experiences at home and at church.

Implications for Ministry

Because two- and three-year-old children are so affected by their surroundings and those who care for them, church facilities should be bright and cheerful and staffed by personnel who model Christian attitudes and actions, and are trained to communicate on the child's level. If preschool facilities at church are homelike, adjustment to it will be easier. The church should supplement the home background and develop positive attitudes toward the Lord and His house.

Workers should establish an atmosphere of calmness in which they can teach spiritual truths and actions related to the child's experience. One adult is needed to work with every four or five children.

Because twos and threes are fearful and somewhat emotionally unstable, those working with this age level should do all that they can to build the children's self-esteem. An atmosphere of security and love is essential with praise given in large doses.

The room should be 25 or 30 square feet for each child. Small rooms and small partitions limit activity and are not conducive to the flexible program twos and threes need. When selecting program materials to use with this age level, they should provide opportunities for self-discovery as well as presentation and application of spiritual concepts.

Summary
Ages two and three are important years. These children's personality structures are being formed and they are impressionable, pliable, and easily guided. Although preschool children are physically active, they tire easily. Intellectually, they discover much through the five senses but are limited in self-expression. Emotionally, they fear the unfamiliar and need an atmosphere of security, love, and individual attention. Socially, they like to play alone and the self-centeredness may make their personalities appear negative at times. Spiritually, these children learn more through attitude than concept and need much repetition in basic facts related to familiar everyday experiences.

Notes
1. R. J. Havighurst, *Human Development and Education* (New York: David McKay Co., 1953), p. 18-25.
2. Grace Craig, *Human Development*, 5th ed. (Englewood Cliffs, NJ: Prentice-Hall, 1989), p. 37.
3. Robert E. Slavin, *Educational Psychology Theory Into Practice*, 2nd ed. (Englewood Cliffs, NJ: Prentice-Hall, 1988), p. 39.

Discussion Questions
1. Why is preschool education being emphasized today?
2. Which key words describe twos and threes in their total personality?
3. How would a preschool age child's concept of life differ from yours?
4. What are some of the preschool child's physical needs?

5. Why is it sometimes difficult to communicate with a preschool child?
6. What spiritual concepts are twos and threes ready to grasp?
7. How can an adult working with this age level communicate spiritual truth on the children's level?

Application Activities

1. In what ways is your church providing opportunities for development of preschoolers?
2. Observe a preschool child for a period of time, keeping notes of your observations on his/her physical, intellectual, emotional, social, and spiritual characteristics.
3. What would you do with a preschool child who stamps his/her feet violently, shakes his/her head, and shouts "no" when you ask him/her to sit with the other children so you can tell a story.
4. Visit the preschool department in your church. Evaluate the room, equipment, personnel, and program as to strengths and areas of possible improvement.
5. Ask a two- or three-year-old child a number of questions about spiritual truth. Note how you have to change your questions in order for the child to be able to respond.
6. Clip pictures of preschoolers from magazines for a "Preschool Photo Album." Give each picture a caption which represents a characteristic of the preschool child.

NEW
EXPERIENCES

EARLY CHILDHOOD

Ages 4 and 5

4

The period from infancy to early childhood, although gradual, is definite. The bodies of four- and five-year-old children lengthen. Their interests widen. Their minds deepen.

It takes a series of little steps to cover the big step of being four on the stairway of learning. The boisterous, intense, talkative, imaginative, and responsive four gradually is beginning to be what five will become. Docile, delightful five is still taking little steps in his growth to cover the interesting step of being five. It's a wonderful age to enjoy, for a tumultuous year looms ahead. [1]

Many fours and fives have participated in early childhood educational experiences either in day care programs, nursery school, or kindergarten. They have learned basic skills in language and socialization. Some children have attended church-related settings in which they have received basic spiritual instruction and have had some opportunity to apply what they have learned. Television programs for children have also expanded knowledge and skills. Therefore, many fours and fives may be more sophisticated in educational experiences before they begin formal schooling and those who work with fours and fives need to build on these foundations.

Developmental Tasks
The accomplishment of these tasks will be signs of developmental progress:

Recognition of sex differences.

Ability to socialize and relate emotionally to others.

Increased ability to express themselves verbally and to communicate with others.

Ability to distinquish between right and wrong. [2]

Physically — *Players*

Four- and five-year-old children are players and all the world is a playground. Never again will they be able to play as completely uninterrupted by other interests. This playtime is more than physical. It also affects their intellectual, social, and spiritual development.

Although adults may think of play as a waste of time, children actually learn many things through constructive play activities. Sensory play teaches children facts about their bodies, senses, and the qualities of things in the environment. Children play with motion through activities such as running, jumping, and skipping. Rough-and-tumble play teaches children how to handle their feelings, to control their impulses, and to filter out negative behaviors which may be inappropriate.

Children play with language to learn rhythm, create new meanings, and to practice and master grammar and words they are learning. Dramatic play and modeling encourages children to take on roles or models to understand social relationships, rules, and various aspects of culture. Games, rituals, and competitive play activities teach children how to take turns, set up guidelines about what is appropriate, and to develop cognitive skills. [3]

Imitative play stimulates children's minds. They remember best what they learn in this way. Four- and five-year-olds normally imitate people, animals, or objects—whatever or whoever impresses them. They may pretend to be a train, a father, a spaceman, a cat, a horse, a policeman, a soldier. These imitations vary with the events, things, and people they see and they can be annoying, but these activities are vital to their personality development.

Develop Rapidly

During early childhood, arms and legs enlarge providing a need for these children to run constantly. Their rate of development is fast at four, slower at five. The varied development of their larger muscles may make them unable to do coordinated activities as well as other children near their age. Even a month difference in age may be significant at this time, for the smaller muscles are beginning to develop causing them to tire readily of intricate projects. Play activities can help the large and small muscles to develop.

Those working with this age level should utilize the four- and five-year-old children's stored-up energy and encourage muscular development through carefully chosen activities. They should alternate active and quiet activities.

Have Limited Energy

Four- and five-year-olds usually have delicate health and contract communicable diseases easily especially when they begin kindergarten. Their growing bodies need sufficient rest and a proper diet. They should not be forced to play or join strenuous activities when they do not feel well.

Intellectually — *Questioners*

The infant discoverer becomes the child questioner. The discovery of these children's enlarged world leads them to ask never-ending questions. As infants they solved their problems by activities. Now that they can talk, the question is their foremost method of learning. Too often parents and other adults suppress these questions and in the process hinder a natural quest for both knowledge and expression.

The educational process begins with questions and continues with the parent or others working with this age level answering these questions directly and fully. "Over answering" can confuse small children and is unnecessary for learning.

Are Developing Self-Identity

Four- and five-year-old children are beginning to recognize themselves as unique persons. These children need to realize that God has made them special people different from everyone else. Parents and those ministering to fours and fives need to help these children accept themselves as they are. Foundations for a positive self-image need to be laid carefully.

Have Increased Vocabulary

The conversation of fours and fives increases as they learn to express themselves through a growing vocabulary. Their vocabularies depend on their home background, television viewing, school, and church contacts; but on the average, their vocabularies consist of 500 to 1500 words.

Adults can ascertain their limitations in vocabulary by asking these children what a word means or encouraging them to use new words in conversation.

Have Limited Concept Understanding

The limited concepts of time, space, and numbers may be springboards for questions. The concepts of fours and fives often are limited. As a result, they might comment after a few minutes of boring waiting: "Mommy, isn't it time to go yet? We have been waiting for hours!"

Distances seem very far to them. After traveling a few miles or blocks they say: "When are we going to be there? We have been riding nearly all day!"

If number concepts are used, the parent may say: "You, daddy, and I are going and that's all." If many people are going, the parent may say: "Many of us are going—our family, Billy and his mother and father, Mary and her mother and father, and a lot of other people."

Talk Freely

Four- and five-year-old children talk freely. They may tell people outside the family things about their home life that would shock their parents. These children often use questions to initiate a conversation. Some typical questions are: Can rabbits jump over a badminton net? Is a house as tall as a giant? Why doesn't Jesus make grandma well?

Have Keen Imagination

The curiosity and keen imagination of four- and five-year-old children are outstanding characteristics. They think mainly in mental pictures. Through play these pictures become real. This gives them the self-confidence of experience to take the initiative in later life. Many poets, artists, and inventors were children with strong imaginations.

Intellectually, according to Piagetian theory, fours and fives are still in the stage whereby they cannot think through the consequences of a particular chain of events. Though these children have made great strides in the use of their language skills, they still judge things by their appearance, think in specifics, and see only one aspect of a total situation. Their thinking is overly concrete and they do not understand symbols or abstractions. They cannot do reversible thinking. They are also self-centered and limited in their ability to classify and categorize.

Emotionally — *Responders*

Four- and five-year-old children are emotionally intense. Their reactions are unpredictable. They may express themselves in colorful or even obnoxious ways, because they think they will get attention.

Can Control Emotions

Four- and five-year-old children can control their emotions more than twos and threes but they still are learning to live with others and need guidance and help. They must learn to avoid unacceptable behavior such as biting, hitting, pinching, and shoving—actions designed to get attention. If all children this age receive the attention they need in a positive way, they will be helped as individuals to gain self-control.

Fear Many Things

These children may be afraid of the unknown, the new, the dark, thunder and lightning, barking dogs, and strange people. These fears are learned from family and friends but they are real for these children and should be recognized. Their fears should not be used to frighten them. Such statements as "I'll lock you in the dark closet" have no place in guiding fours and fives.

Show Jealousy

Children at four or five may be jealous. Parents sometimes unknowingly cause this by lack of attention, especially when a new baby arrives. Jealousy may be shown by biting or hitting the new baby. Wise parents carefully prepare four- and five-year-olds for the arrival of a new brother or sister and let them share in loving care.

Socially — *Conformists*

Socially, four- and five-year-old children are beginning to develop group consciousness, are overcoming their self-centeredness, and may be showing some leadership ability.

Are Developing Group Consciousness

Four- and five-year-old children conform to others. They now add many outsiders to their previously limited home acquaintances. They are also more familiar with their surroundings and communicate better. They enjoy being with children their own age but are still quite self-centered. This may cause them to be timid and afraid of children who are new to them or be reluctant to join group activities.

Four- and five-year-olds soon learn that self-centeredness and stubbornness may mean separation from the group. As tantrums and tears fail, they cooperate with the group so they can be accepted. In this way they learn teamwork.

Are Overcoming Self-Centeredness

Fours and fives may want to be first, the biggest, or the winner. Although it is good for them to learn to compete effectively, they need to abide by the rules and restrictions of others. As their contacts with other children increase, they overcome some of their self-centeredness.

Have Leadership Ability

Leadership abilities are emerging on a very limited basis. Group activities provide opportunity for these children to lead by having them stand before the group to lead a song or story play. Show-and-tell and other expressive activities also encourage leadership development.

Erikson describes children at age four or five as being in the stage of initiative versus guilt. Children explore beyond themselves through the use of their maturing motor and language skills. They begin to discover how the world works and what they can do to affect it. They realize the world has both real and imaginary people and things.

Hopefully, they will learn to deal with things and people in constructive ways, and accept without guilt that certain things are not allowed. They require confirmation from adults that their initiative is accepted and that their contributions are truly valued, even if they seem insignificant. Children at this stage can begin to gain a strong sense of initiative. If they are criticized severely or punished, however, they may begin to feel guilty for many of their own actions and carry these guilt feelings into later life. [4]

Spiritually — *Believers*

Parents and those ministering to fours and fives can easily influence children at this age. They believe everything they are told. It is important to be absolutely truthful in answering these children's questions and not take advantage of their trusting spirit. They need to realize that adults also are limited in knowledge even though they have lived much longer than they have.

Confuse Reality and Imagination

The undependable memory of four- and five-year-old children may cause them to confuse details in reality with the make-believe world because of an overstimulated imagination and the inability to distinguish fact from fiction or truth from error. Those who work with these children should realize that a child not being fully truthful may result from exaggeration or inaccuracy.

Possibly these children have overheard their parents speak in superlative terms so frequently that they have formed the habit. To make an impression, they tell stories that are exaggerated.

Sometimes the inaccurate replies of fours and fives are partly due to inattention or forgetfulness. Unable to answer accurately, they give the easiest answer that occurs to them.

At this age children seldom deliberately lie unless they find it profitable. They may begin lying regularly when they find that their act was not discovered or that they are overly punished if they confess.

When a child lies, adults should encourage him/her to confess the lie, and to be truly sorry for telling it. Adults have great responsibility in being truthful. Their example will influence these children more than anything else. It is a good policy to teach children the biblical consequence of lying and the happiness that comes from telling the truth.

When children exaggerate, encourage them to return to reality by saying, "That was a play story, wasn't it? Now tell me what really happened."

Think of God as a Real Person

Four- and five-year-old children have a simple faith and trust in God and in Jesus. They have no difficulty thinking of God as a real person. They do not need to be convinced of the existence of God, but simply believe that God is. They talk with God or Jesus as a real person, even as they express themselves to adults.

These children can come to love God as they come to love those in their homes. They may not fully understand God as sovereign, but they can experience and express gratitude, love, and reverence.

The praises and prayers of fours and fives should be in language they can understand and should express their own feelings. Their prayer life should lead them to express thanks as well as ask for things.

Have Growing Spiritual Concepts

The church and its ministry to fours and fives in whatever the setting should center its teaching around the Word of God and help these children grasp simple Bible truths. Learning activities should help fours and fives with meaningful spiritual concepts such as God is the heavenly Father and creator, and Jesus is his loving Son. Learning activities can be correlated with the seasons, providing materials appropriate to spring, summer, autumn, and winter. At these times, fours and fives can build a treasury of meaningful concepts that show the world as God's world.

Are Developing Self-Control

Discipline is an important responsibility of the home. Parental authority comes from God (Ex. 20:1-17). Parents should realize their role as representatives of God and understand the seriousness of teaching self-control. Punishment, as a part of discipline, should be administered for the good of the children and for the glory of God.

"He who spares the rod hates his son, but he who loves him is careful to discipline him" (Prov. 13:24). While this passage has been misinterpreted and misused, it includes constructive effort to guide children in the right direction and teach them self-control.

Discipline includes forgiveness, love, and affection. Parents should not restrict their children to narrow patterns of behavior, but furnish them with a framework of biblical principles which will be a foundation in biblical self-discipline.

Have Limited Sense of Right and Wrong

In developing concepts about morality (which has to do with the sense of right and wrong), fours and fives appear to be at the first level referred to by Lawrence Kohlberg. This level is composed of two stages. In stage one children obey rules in order to avoid punishment. At the second stage, children obey to obtain rewards or to have favors returned.

It is important to remember that Kohlberg emphasized that moral judgment can be taught, but we cannot assume a child's behavior will change as a result of knowing what is right or wrong. Even adults have far more knowledge than they act upon. Because fours and fives are just beginning to develop in their thinking processes, their moral judgments will likely be very limited, basic, and concrete. [5]

Implications for Ministry

Spiritual development of children frequently is shared by home and church. Parents remain the greatest of all teachers and cannot afford to relinquish their place to others. The church should assist the home in the spiritual development of children and supplement and reinforce teaching done in the home. If the home is not Christian, the church should reach the parents with the gospel and help them realize their responsibility in their children's spiritual training.

Those working with this age level should be alert to answer the many questions of four- and five-year-olds naturally. They should cultivate their desire for learning and carefully lay a spiritual foundation.

These children should be taught about God's loving care and his Son, Jesus. Learning activities should emphasize Bible stories which are on the children's level and within their experience. The church and home need to work together to develop the potential of fours and fives.

Summary

Four- and five-year-old children are players physically. Play opens doors for them to develop their total personality. Intellectually, they learn rapidly through questioning. This stimulates their thinking, enriches their background, broadens their understanding. The emotions of these children may be intense but are improved over the pre-school years. They may fear the new and unfamiliar and need help in adjusting. Socially, these children conform, are group conscious, and begin to develop leadership abilities. Self-centeredness may be apparent. Spiritually, they believe what they are told. This leaves those ministering to this age level with a great responsibility to be honest.

Notes

1. Eleanor Doan and Lois Curley, *Teaching Fours-N-Fives Successfully* (Glendale, CA: Gospel Light Publications, 1963), p. 9.
2. R. J. Havighurst, *Human Development and Education* (New York: David McKay Co., 1953), pp. 9-17.
3. Grace Craig, *Human Development,* 5th ed. (Englewood Cliffs, NJ: Prentice-Hall, 1989), pp. 255, 256.
4. Anita E. Woolfolk, *Educational Psychology,* 3rd ed. (Englewood Cliffs, NJ: Prentice-Hall, 1987), p. 91.
5. Craig, pp. 352, 353.

Discussion Questions

1. What key words can be used to describe the total personality development of fours and fives?
2. Give several reasons why play is so important in the development of fours and fives.
3. What guidelines should be applied in handling a child's questions?
4. What actions characterize the emotional development of the four- and five-year-old child?
5. How do fours or fives learn to adjust with others?
6. What spiritual concepts should be taught to fours and fives?
7. What specific guidelines should be considered when teaching spiritual concepts to these children?

Application Activities

1. Prepare a list of learning activities which can contribute to the total development of the four- or five-year-old child. Which would be most appropriate for home? For the church? Other settings?
2. Plan to interview a teacher of fours and fives. To prepare for the interview write up a list of questions you want to ask about the key characteristics and needs of these children. Organize your questions under the five areas of personality development. Prepare a brief summary report.
3. Make a list of some of the biblical beliefs we have as adults that are given in the church doctrinal statement. Take three or four of these concepts and try to explain them so fours and fives can understand. Use simple vocabulary and sentence structure they can grasp. Evaluate the process. Was the task easy? Why? What problems did you encounter? What would help you to improve in the process of communicating spiritual truth to them?

HORIZONS BROADEN

MIDDLE CHILDHOOD

Ages 6-8

5

There is no sharp transition between early and middle childhood, but the entire span (ages 6-8) is a continuing transition period. These children progress from home to school, play to work, imagination to reason. In the midst of these transitions, they add friends and assume more definite responsibilities. Those working with this age level must keep in mind the great difference in ability between the 6, 7, and 8 year old.

Developmental Tasks

During middle childhood the following progress should be achieved:
Physical skills necessary to common childhood games.
Establishment of wholesome attitudes toward self.
Compatability with age-mates.
Adjustment to boy-girl social role.
Development of fundamental language and computational skills.
Building of a recognizable set of values.
Balance of personal independence and relationship to established groups. [1]

Physically — *Hustlers*

While six- to eight-year-old children can maintain attention and interest for a span of ten to fifteen minutes, their restless nature leads to ceaseless activity. This furthers growth and development.

Grow Unevenly

Although six- to eight-year-old children seek strenuous activity, they tire easily. Growth is uneven for them and their hearts do not grow in proportion to the rest of the body. These children will not readily admit that they are tired and need to rest. Adults should be alert to physical limitations and provide alternate periods of activity and rest. Also, they need a proper balanced diet to develop a healthy body. They may contact contagious diseases because of their expanding world of friends and this low resistance.

Are Developing Finer Muscle Coordination

Increased awareness of the senses and control of muscular action enables greater perception and accuracy of movement. Moving their larger muscles in walking, running, climbing, throwing, becomes almost automatic. They are freed for mental growth and so they advance both mentally and physically. Programs with much activity are needed for them to develop muscular control and coordination. Six- to eight-year-old children literally struggle in developing their finer muscles. They lack coordination and do not have much staying power. Projects must be chosen carefully so they do not become too frustrated and give up in the process.

Lose Teeth

Six- to eight-year-old children will lose their temporary teeth. Some children get their permanent teeth earlier than others. As children begin to lose their teeth, they need reassurance that this is a natural process.

Are Developing Eye-Hand Coordination

One of the reasons children at this age level are able to begin the process of learning to read and write more readily is that their eye-hand coordination is improving. Hence, the 6-year-old child will experience more difficulty and the finished product might be crude. Perfection should not be emphasized at this level.

Eight-year-olds will have much improved eye-hand coordination and are capable of reading and writing more precisely. Reading problems may develop if children are having difficulty in coordination.

Are More Selective In Activities

Girls tend to be ahead of boys in their development during early and middle childhood, particularly in their physical and intellectual development. Girls may do better in academics, and boys may have more difficulty sitting still because of their need for activity. Boys are likely to be more aggressive than girls and like to roughhouse. Girls seem to have better coordination in finer muscular development and may do better at tasks which require use of the finer muscles.

Differences also are more noticeable in play activities. Many boys will include in their play vigorous scrimmages and scrambles. Their handcrafts may include kites, boats, spaceships, and miniature cars while the girls may prefer dolls, miniature house furniture, art, and music.

Many of the differences in sex roles are due to cultural expectations of masculine and feminine behavior. Parents expect male children to be "real boys"—and females to be "real girls." Fathers particularly seem to teach specific gender roles by reinforcing femininity in daughters and masculinity in sons.

The learning of sex roles begins in infancy. More rigid stereotypes develop by the time children are in the middle childhood years. Parents and others working with this age level need to be careful not to stereotype children or activities. Many activities can be used effectively with both sexes. It is more important to emphasize the development of individual personalities, interests, and skills in sex role behavior. [2]

Intellectually — *Observers*

As six- to eight-year-old children mature, they observe more closely, even noticing things the mentally-absorbed adult misses. They do not understand these new sights and scenes as their reasoning and discrimination are just awakening. It is easy to overestimate their intellectual progress at this time; but the keen interest and search for information is refreshing.

Think Literally

Six- to eight-year-old children still think literally. Generalizations, abstractions, and symbols are easily misunderstood. To them, a light is a bulb or something that helps them see. They do not think of Jesus as the spiritual light of the world. Because of the limitations of their literal interpretations, they are helped by teaching which includes questions for clarification and understanding.

Live in the Here and Now

Because these children relate to the here and now, often they are limited in their understanding of time, space, and number concepts. As they move into such subjects as geography, history, and mathematics, they may learn to repeat facts without understanding the material.

Children understand new concepts by relating each new experience to previous knowledge. The Lord constantly referred to well-known facts in teaching new truths.

People who understand children's experiences can communicate best with them. Children often learn from their peers because they understand each other. Adults must explore children's lives with genuine interest, concern, and love before they understand them sufficiently to utilize the principles of association in teaching them.

A helpful relationship between parents and other adults who are working with their son/daughter often helps clarify the child's attitudes. A visit to the school will help both parents and other adults working with children of this age level to familiarize themselves with experiences through which the children pass. These contacts provide excellent aids for presenting spiritual truths as there is opportunity.

Memorize More Easily

These children are able to memorize more quickly and easily and are ready to learn verses with references. They also like to learn songs, poems, and other materials. They are beginning to think chronologically and sequentially. They realize that the Bible is a complete book with two major divisions and many smaller parts. Older children in this age group are able to learn the names of the Bible books in their proper order.

How much children at this age retain of memorized information will depend on how well they are taught, the application of the content to their daily life, and on how often the content is reviewed and reinforced. Those who work with this age group need to emphasize the practical importance of Scripture memorization— that it can keep us from sin (Ps. 119:11) and can be helpful in encouraging and comforting us. It is better for these children to master several verses or passages and their meanings well than to memorize many things and soon forget them. Audiovisuals, careful explanations, and opportunities to practice the truth are essentials in effective memorization.

Are Beginning to Think Concretely

Intellectually, according to Piaget, these children are beginning to think and reason more concretely and logically. They are beginning to classify and categorize things. They can also arrange items in sequence and are beginning to reverse processes. They can also theorize about the world. They think about and anticipate what will happen, make guesses or estimates, and then experiment to test the outcomes. They are able to see things in the context of other meanings and deal with part-to-whole relationships.

In this stage of development, as children explore their physical environment, they ask themselves questions and find the answers, and in time, acquire a more complex, sophisticated form of thinking.

These children's understanding of symbolism and abstractions is still limited unless these concepts are related to physical objects or events. In relation to spiritual truth, they have difficulty making the transfer from literal and concrete objects to spiritual meanings. For example, one cannot assume these children understand the spiritual significance of "Jesus is the door" or "Jesus is the Light of the world" without careful explanation of the spiritual meaning based on a concrete object. [3]

Emotionally — *Insecure*

Six- to eight-year-old children have easily stimulated emotions, "feel deeply" with others, and quickly express how they feel. They are quite insecure in their personality development. These insecurities may be related to the fact that their world view is broadening and they are in the process of making many transitions. They are confronting new experiences in school and in other situations and are not sure how to handle them.

Being away from their parents for continually longer periods, these children are ever coping with the unknown. Often emotionally insecure, they may express themselves in childish behavior. This is part of their maturing process. Patience and understanding may help them overcome the insecurities which lead to emotional outburst and cause them to express themselves in ways unacceptable to adults.

Desire Adult Approval

These children are sometimes referred to as "the pleasers." They will do whatever they can to secure approval from adults. They thrive on honest praise and accomplishments and are quick to recognize when what they do is truly appreciated.

Are Concerned About Others

These children are especially interested in those their own age, but show sympathy and concern for all ages. This emotional outlet can be channeled into service projects for the elderly, for those in need, and for children of missionaries.

Socially — *Friendly*

Six- to eight-year-old children make friends and converse easily, especially with those interested in them. In their effort to please those ministering to them, they may arrive early or stay afterward to help. Often the pleasure of a friendly personal visit is abundant reward for such help. Times like these give opportunity to encourage children in establishing good interpersonal relationships.

Participate in Groups

These children want the group to accept them and treat them as equals. If guided to acceptable behavior standards, they will be helped toward acceptance by their peers as a part of the group. Group participation helps the individual child bypass the frustrations caused by revealing unperfected skills which are seen when participating alone.

Prefer Cooperative Rather Than Competitive Activities

Six- to eight-year-olds often dislike competition and would rather work with other children at their own level of development. Boys and girls play well together, although sex antagonism may begin to develop during this period. Some organizations separate the boys from the girls. When men and women, or couples, work with this age, they provide the wholesome image of both men and women being interested in spiritual matters, as well as introduce variety in leadership.

Are in Industry Versus Inferiority Stage

According to Erikson, six- to eight-year-old children are entering the industry versus inferiority stage in social development. This stage is characterized by the conviction "I am what I learn...Success brings a sense of industry, a good feeling about oneself and one's abilities. Failure, on the other hand, creates a negative self-image, a sense of inadequacy that may hinder future learning." [4]

These children may discover pleasure in perseverance and being productive through industry, or they may feel they cannot measure up to their own standards or those of teachers, parents, or siblings. The neighborhood, school, and peer interaction become increasingly important, while the influence of parents may decrease as these children assess their own worth. The role of adult Christians can become significant in assisting these children in making a transition from home to the outside world.

Spiritually — *Discerners*

At this age level, children are God-inclined, with a tender conscience, a strong impulse to obey, and implicit faith. They still believe what they are told, but are already beginning to seek proof and certainty.

Distinguish Differences

These children are still eager for a story. But because life is becoming real, stories are now followed with the invariable question: "Is it really true?" Accounts of Santa Claus and fairy tales are questioned and rejected. If Bible stories are presented with extra-biblical embellishments, these, too, will be disregarded. Stories true to the Word, however, lay the foundation for a chronological study of the Bible later and should be labeled as "true."

These children also discover there are good and bad associations likely to affect their own character. They experience moral failure and realize their own weaknesses. Their right and wrong acts affect their own peace and happiness. Parents and other adults working with this age level should emphasize the need for choosing the right and rejecting the wrong.

Are Developing Moral Reasoning

Some of these children may be in the first stage of Kohlberg's Level 1 of moral development—punishment and obedience orientation. Judgment is based on personal needs and others' rules. The rules are obeyed to avoid punishment. Others may have moved to the second stage, personal reward orientation—what's right is whatever satisfies one's own needs and occasionally the needs of others.

Still others may be entering Level 2 of moral development where judgment is based on approval by others, family expectations, traditional values, and laws of society. Stage 3 emphasizes good boy-nice girl orientation— good behavior is whatever pleases or helps others and is approved by them. One earns approval by being nice. [5]

Are Forming Values

An adult's ability to attract children is a dynamic teaching tool, for children imitate the doer rather than the deed. Winning children to Christ is more often achieved by a person with a winning personality. Parent's and other adults' values become their standard of values, the measure of their conduct, and the scope of their conscience. Conscientious children often are found in an atmosphere wherein "whatever is lovely, whatever is admirable" (Phil. 4:8) are conveyed spontaneously. These children may not be able to define their value system verbally; but their attitudes will affect their behavior in years to come.

These children distinguish between what is taught by precept and what is taught by practice. They are frustrated by contradictions and cannot understand deceiving the ticket agent about their age to reduce a fare.

Parents and other adults working with this age level may sin by what they neglect as well as by what they do. It is difficult to teach children to pray if influential adults don't. If at the family devotional time children see and hear parents pray as they have been taught to do, they quickly learn to do the same.

In church and Sunday school attendance also, actions speak loudly. Parents who urge their children to attend services and will not go themselves may end their children's interest in church-going rather than establishing it.

Can Understand Salvation and Receive Christ as Savior

The readiness of six- to eight-year-olds for spiritual decision depends upon previous home experiences, attendance at church, meaningful teaching, and personal application of the Word of God.

They can understand the salvation message if it is presented simply and concretely. Romans 3:10 and 3:23 may help them realize they are sinners. Then John 1:12 and 3:16 will show them that they can join God's family by receiving the Lord Jesus as their Savior. These children, in their desire for acceptance, may falsely indicate a decision, so they should not be pushed to premature actions.

Parents and other adults ministering to this age level need to work together in a follow-up program of spiritual nurture and growth, which begins immediately after children receive Christ.

Worship Simply and Sincerely

The capacity of these children to know God increases as their world enlarges and experience broadens. Even though they cannot comprehend God as adults can, their worship of God, as an unseen companion and a faithful friend, should be encouraged. They should talk freely to God thanking Him for the many blessings He gives such as health, home, and friends.

A worship service can be meaningful to these children if it is planned on their level. Many of these children love and understand the privilege of meeting God through worship. They should learn the meaning of the various segments of the worship service. Religious holidays should be associated not only with friends and close relatives, but also with Christ Himself.

These children benefit by worship on their own level through Sunday school worship services, the children's church program, and the vacation Bible school. In addition, when the home provides a time for family worship in which children participate and help plan, six- to eight-year-olds better learn to thank the Lord, sing, and share their understanding of the Word of God.

If these children are to have a right attitude in spiritual matters, good first impressions are important. Group and class experiences of worship can be helped by an orderly program, atmosphere, and arrangement of furnishings which produce a deep feeling of respect.

Implications for Ministry

The church program should provide opportunities for six- to eight-year-old children to assume responsibilities, helping them overcome insecurity in adjusting to new situations. They need special love, attention, and patience.

These children should be encouraged to memorize Scripture and songs and to participate in group activities. They should also have opportunities to help serve through learning activities or church outreach in the community.

The plan of salvation needs to be presented clearly and consistently with individual counsel and follow-up. These children understand basic spiritual truths and can apply Bible content to their daily experiences if is is presented on their level. When they have received Christ as Savior, they should be encouraged to witness to others.

Summary

Six- to eight-year-old children seldom have a dull moment! This is a period of transition with these children adjusting from home life to school life. They are away from home more, like to feel grown-up, and seek approval from adult leadership. Physically, they are strenuously active but tire easily because of uneven growth. Intellectually, they are alert and increasing their vocabulary. They understand more about time, space, and number concepts and have a more dependable memory. They can memorize well if challenged. Often they are emotionally insecure and need special affection and guidance from adults. Socially, these children are friendly and enjoy being with both boys and girls their own age. They appreciate cooperative activities without individual competition. Spiritual discerners, they distinguish fact from fancy, notice the difference between right and wrong, and recognize inconsistencies. They may be ready to receive Christ as Savior. They learn many of the basic spiritual concepts through storytelling. They are capable of heartfelt worship and need to be taught reverence for the Lord, His Word, and His House.

Notes

1. R. J. Havighurst, *Human Development and Education* (New York: David McKay Co., 1953), pp.25-51.
2. Grace Craig, *Human Development*, 5th ed. (Englewood Cliffs, NJ: Prentice-Hall, 1989), pp. 77-79.
3. Craig, pp. 306-309.
4. Robert E. Slavin, *Educational Psychology Theory Into Practice*, 2nd ed. (Englewood Cliffs, NJ: Prentice-Hall, 1988), p. 40.
5. Anita E. Woolfolk, *Educational Psychology*, 3rd ed. (Englewood Cliffs, NJ: Prentice-Hall, 1987), p. 110.

Discussion Questions

1. Why is middle childhood considered a transition period?
2. Describe this child physically, intellectually, emotionally, socially, spiritually, using one key word for each.
3. How do these children's play activities differ from those of four- and five-year-old children?
4. How can you help this age child overcome insecurity?
5. What spiritual emphases should be taught at this level?
6. How would you explain the plan of salvation to six- to eight-year-olds?
7. How would you explain to this age child the meaning of "Let Jesus come into your heart"?
8. How can you help children of this age level who have received Christ as Savior to begin to grow in their Christian lives?

Application Activities

1. Develop a list of the characteristics of six- to eight-year-old children. Then visit a ministry in your church in which these children are being taught and observe how they evidence characteristics similar to your list. How do you account for the differences in characteristics among children of the same age?
2. Interview the teachers in your middle childhood department. Ask at least three teachers what they consider to be important personality characteristics the teacher of this age level needs. What characteristics would you add?
3. Write a step by step procedure you could use in leading a six- to eight-year-old child to Christ as Savior. For each step identify and explain a Scripture verse which would be appropriate.

PERSONIFIED EXUBERANCE

LATER CHILDHOOD

Ages 9-11

6

Few periods of development are as challenging to children or to those who work with them as later childhood. These children are usually coordinated and abundantly active and seem never to lose their zest for living. These exuberant preadolescents need a firm relationship with the Lord and wise spiritual guidance to adjust to the years ahead.

Developmental Tasks

During later childhood, the following should be experienced:
Steady physical growth.
Perfecting of skills begun in middle childhood such as compatability with age-mates, recognition of moral and spiritual values, basics in language and computational skills.
Healthy attitudes toward social groups and institutions.
Wholesome attitudes toward themselves.

Physically — *Abundant Energy*

Nine- to 11-year-olds usually enjoy excellent health and slower, steady growth. They are ready to go the limit in any activity. They delight in challenges and crave excitement and physical exploits. They become personally involved and seek self-achievement in physical development.

Overflow with Energy

These children seem never to tire but overflow with energy. They run through buildings, twist in their seats, slam the door. They follow enthusiastic leaders who enjoy life to its fullest. Increased strength enable these children to be relatively free from disease. They need a balanced diet as their appetites increase and also plenty of fresh air, sunshine, and rest.

They need varied activities and experiences, especially outdoors. Summer and winter camping programs also provide opportunity for relating truths about God. Through outdoor activities they discover God's laws and develop an appreciation for God as creator. This can lead these children to dedicate their lives to Christ.

Are Developing Physical Coordination

Nine- to 11-year-olds grow steadier and improve their physical coordination. They accept more challenging physical tasks and can complete intricate projects. Goals should challenge them, yet be attainable. They need to be encouraged to finish what they begin and do acceptable work in whatever they undertake. This will help them develop the self-control necessary to progress toward more difficult tasks.

Neglect Proper Physical Care

These children may become so involved in living that they neglect proper physical care. They need to learn appropriate grooming and how to care for personal possessions and their rooms. Typically they will toss their clothes and other items anywhere in their room and say they cleaned it. Learning neatness may seem impossible but they can and will learn these important lessons of self-discipline and awareness of others.

Their abounding energy and excellent health can be channeled into worthwhile activities. It is helpful to contact them outside the church setting and share in their overall development so that they may become a "doer of the Word and not a hearer only" (James 1:22).

Intellectually — *Investigative*

Nine- to 11-year-olds observe more accurately than younger children and reason more logically. They are more self-reliant and become inquisitive explorers. They are discovering answers to their many questions. They are alert and eager to learn anything new. While they enjoy contests they are not dependent upon this kind of motivation to learn.

According to Piaget's theory, these children have advanced in their reasoning capacities and are capable of doing more in-depth thinking than younger children. They classify, categorize, and manipulate mental data with more ease and greater skill. They can estimate, theorize, and master logical operations; but they think concretely and literally.

Symbols and abstractions can be taught with familiar examples, concrete props, and visual aids. Those ministering to this age level must not assume children understand these concepts without explanation. Skillful questioning, careful listening, and paying close attention to the ways these children try to solve problems will teach us a great deal about how they think and learn. [1]

Are Collectors

The investigative spirit of nine- to 11-year-old children leads them to numerous enterprises, one being collecting items. Collections often include books, sports cards, stamps, coins, stones, models, miniatures, butterflies, shells. When there is guidance, collections serve useful purposes. Observation and judgment are quickened, foundations are laid for organized study, and lifelong habits can be formed. Discussing collections, trading, and sharing also develops interpersonal relationships and communication abilities.

Learn by Discovery

These children are inquisitive and investigative. They are interested in how things are put together and how they work. They ask many thought-provoking questions. They may even question the authority of adults. Good clear answers based on the facts are essential, though at times adults may need to respond, "I don't know," rather than give a vague or incorrect answer.

These children are capable of doing simple inductive Bible studies based on questions about the text. They can discover with adult guidance what the Bible says and how to apply it to their lives.

Are Perfecting Reading Skills

Nine- to 11-year-old children read more easily and enter a new, larger world of books. How far these children explore these new horizons often depends on their homes, friends, schools, and churches. Unfortunately, many of them have not developed their reading skills well. Reading problems usually begin to surface during third and fourth grades. Many children at this age may spend several hours watching television each week and become passive in mastering reading skills. Parents and other adults working with this age level need to do whatever they can to encourage them to develop good reading habits.

Provision of good books through a circulating church library can provide these children with much thought for spiritual growth. At times church library books can be brought directly to learning and socialization situations to enable easy selection.

At home, time should be provided for developing good reading habits. This also necessitates a supply of suitable reading materials. Often a planned visit to the library by parents and children will stimulate their interest in books. Book-loving parents and other adults ministering to this age level create book-loving children and influence the kind of books they read. Christian literature provided by home and church is a mighty spiritual force in shaping lives for God. The church and home can also work together to help these children explore the Book of Books, the Bible, for themselves.

Think Logically

Nine- to 11-year-olds are beginning to realize how things and events fit together. They understand the laws of sequence and consequence and have a historical and chronological sense of time, space, location, and distance. They are interested in current events.

Older children are curious about Bible geography and history and ready to consider the "why" of people's actions and God's dealings.

Have an Excellent Memory

Later childhood is often called the golden age of memory. If memorization is interesting, these children will be motivated to meaningful memorization and understand what they memorize. If so, they frequently apply the meaning of the verse to their own lives.

Since these children are more skillful in their abilities and can compete with others, contests and other motivational devices may be used to increase learning. Those working with this age level, however, must be careful that these children do not compete just for the sake of competing or winning an extrinsic reward. Some children may feel left out because they do not have the intellectual abilities or skills to compete. The results can be damaging to self-esteem and do great harm to children in their total development. The best kind of motivation is that which brings personal satisfaction, progress, and achievement to the individual.

It is important that memory programs be coordinated at this age level. Often those in leadership positions in different ministries all try to encourage children of this age level to memorize Scripture and other materials in their specific ministries. The active participants become overwhelmed with all they have to memorize, and consequently, do not learn anything well or may take a defeatist attitude and give up.

Emotionally — *Expressive*

Children at this age freely release their emotions. They shout, run, and quickly become emotionally involved in boisterous activities. Even when they gain control over their emotions, they display them because of their exuberance. They need to learn when to be serious and quiet, and when to be lighthearted and jovial.

Are Impatient

Although gaining self-control, they are easily excited and on the defensive at the slightest accusation. They are quick to argue but soon cool off. If their wishes are not fulfilled, they become disturbed and say unkind things they do not mean. These children need patience and respect for others' rights and feelings and leaders who respect the children's rights and feelings.

Because of a lack of knowledge, experience, and self-control, these children may arrive at unfounded conclusions, generalize, and condemn others without thinking. They need help to make sound judgments based on factual information. Showing them how to gather facts before they judge will help.

Act Brave

These children like to convince others they are fearless. They may, however, be afraid of the dark, staying alone at night, or engaging in a fight. They need to learn that others also are afraid of some things and that the Lord can help them when they need courage. They also need to realize it is not wrong to be fearful of some things that may be harmful. Drugs and alcohol are two prime examples.

Dislike Displaying Outward Emotions

They do not like sentimental expression nor do they want others to feel sorry for them when they are in trouble. Older boys seem even to resent some outward displays of affection.

A simple "Good night, mom and dad" or "So long" may carry much hidden affection even if it is not evidenced. When these children express themselves as they desire, they also are realizing that people express themselves differently. Thus they learn to accept varying degrees of emotional expression on the part of others.

Love Humor

Nine- to 11-year-old children are developing a sense of humor and understand cartoons and jokes. They may tell a story and then laugh more loudly than anyone else. They sometimes do not understand the implications of the jokes they tell. They need to realize all things are not funny and not to tell jokes which derogate other people. Parents and other adults working with this age level who enjoy humor themselves and laugh along with these children can help them learn good humor and to evaluate a humorous story in the light of biblical principles.

Socially — *Adjusting*

Being more capable physically and able to think independently, children at this age begin to seek independence from adult leadership. Within limitations, liberty to act independently will help them prepare for adolescence.

According to Erikson's theory, these children are in the same stage of social development as six- to eight-year-old children— industry versus inferiority. They are more aware of their strengths and weaknesses, and may develop low self-esteem if they do not feel they are successful. Parents and other adults working with this age level need to help them develop a positive self-image by accentuating the positive, encouraging and commending them, and teaching them how to compensate for their weaknesses by achieving in what they are able to do well. They need to be taught how to be industrious and productive without having to measure up to adult standards.

Are Joining Social Groups of the Same Sex

These children have advanced in their relationships with others, especially with those of the same sex. The peer group has begun to influence them as much or more than their family. Their adventuresome spirits lead them to seek freedom from home ties. They want to join a group, gang, or club which often is composed of neighborhood, school, or church peers. They like secret codes and passwords.

At times they may rely more on their peer group than their parents and other adults. If they join the wrong kind of gang, problems may develop. This influence may be avoided if a church provides wholesome peer group relationships through club organizations.

Are Antagonistic Toward the Opposite Sex

Boys and girls at this age often tend to be antagonistic toward each other and do not relate well. They segregate themselves in their activities. Behavior problems may be prevalent in mixed groups and the the person in charge may spend more time disciplining children than leading them. Male leadership should be provided for boys and female leadership for girls. Husband-wife teams are ideal in coeducational groupings. These children should have planned social activities together to learn how to respect each other and to learn basic social behaviors.

Sense Fairness and Justice

These children want to be treated as persons. They do not like favoritism but want justice. When they make their own rules, they are usually more strict with themselves and impose severe penalties for any infraction. They may reject the individual who does not follow the group norm.

Enjoy Competition

Nine- to 11-year-old children are able to compete better because of skill development and finer muscular control. They eagerly participate in competitive activities such as Bible drills, contests, and games. Competition, however, should not be overused. These children need to be taught how to cooperate and develop a team spirit. Individuals should be encouraged to compete against themselves as well as with others. If some individuals are insecure in competitive activities, care should be exercised to make them feel part of the group.

Spiritually — *Relating*

Nine- to 11-year-olds identify with people they like and admire. They need worthy examples who maintain high standards and teach respect for proper authority. Consistent action and spiritual vibrancy are important characteristics of adults working with this age group.

Children at this age level admire those who do what they would like to do. They admire people for what they do without thinking about what they are. They choose their heroes from the people they see, read about, or watch on television, and they form their life patterns as they observe the lives of others. They love to mimic, and they reveal their ideals by the persons they imitate. [2]

Worship Heroes

Since these children are hero worshipers, they should be exposed to worthy heroes. All heroes used as examples in learning situations should point them to Christ as their ideal. Great Bible characters, missionaries of history, and church and denominational missionaries can be presented—always pointing to their relationship to Christ.

Are in Prime Time for Salvation

Although children of this age level may already have received Christ, this should not be assumed—even if they have grown up in the church.

Children at this age need God's plan of salvation presented simply and logically. They should identify with Christ and be firmly established in God's Word before the years of adolescence.

Respond to Instruction in Christian Growth

After salvation these children need to grow in Christ. They can grasp serious matters of life. Growth in a knowledge of God's Word and Christian experience will prepare them for their teens.

Nine- to 11-year-olds can understand spiritual concepts, doctrine, Bible chronology, and Christian living when these things are presented on their level. They need systematic teaching with personal application. They are interested in living the truth, but they need good models. They can understand the ministry of the Holy Spirit and should be taught to allow Him to control their lives.

Discern Spiritual Truth

Older children have no difficulty differentiating right from wrong, truth from error. It may be difficult for them to obey the truth even though they have knowledge of biblical concepts. When they do wrong, however, they must learn to confess their sins, seek forgiveness, then move ahead with God. They should learn to accept strength from God, to admit wrong, and to do right. They need the truth taught clearly and plainly and to realize that God has a plan for their lives.

Are Beginning To Do Moral Reasoning

Nine- to 11-year-old children seem to be operating at several levels in Kohlberg's stages of moral reasoning. Some of these children may still be at the level in which judgment is based on personal needs and others' rules. Others are making judgments which are based on others' approval, family expectations, traditional values, the laws of society, and loyalty to country. Naturally, they are concerned about the approval of others, and they also realize the need for respecting authority. Certainly, these children can be taught how to make moral judgments as Kohlberg indicates, but their behaviors may not always be consistent with what they know and have been taught. [3]

Implications for Ministry

Nine- to 11-year-olds need models who are active doers of the Word. Those who work with this age level must be mentally alert and creative, eager to challenge them to their potentials.

Bible study should emphasize discovering God's truth. These children should be challenged to establish a personal devotional life in which they daily read God's Word, spend time in prayer, and feel free to talk about the Lord. They also need challenge to give their lives to Christ.

The church must provide activities for these children to join a social group in which they can be fully accepted.

Summary

Nine- to 11-year-old children are exuberance personfied! Physically, they grow slower and steadier than previously, but they abound in energy and do not tire easily. They are well coordinated and are developing their skills. Intellectually, they are alert and reason well. They want clear answers to their questions. They read more easily and have an excellent memory. Emotionally, they are expressive but may be impatient. They have few fears and enjoy humor. Socially, at times it appears they have an aversion to the opposite sex; but they will study and play together under mature leadership. They like to join groups and clubs whose members are of their own sex. Their skillfulness encourages competition. Spiritually, they are in a prime time for salvation and respond well to Christian growth. They are able to discover and discern truth for themselves. The potential in their lives is unlimited and every opportunity should be used to reach them for Christ.

Notes

1. Anita Woolfolk, *Educational Psychology,* 3rd ed. (Englewood Cliffs, NJ: Prentice-Hall, 1987), pp. 62-67.
2. Marjorie E. Soderholm, *The Junior* (Grand Rapids: Baker Book House, 1968), p. 20.
3. Woolfolk, p. 110.

Discussion Questions

1. How would you describe nine- to 11-year-olds physically?
2. Nine- to 11-year-olds have abounding energy. How would you channel these energies into worthwhile areas?
3. As compared to six- to eight-year olds, how do these children express their emotions?
4. What characteristics are outstanding in the social life of these children?
5. What are some of the spiritual needs adults working with this age level can meet in these children's lives?
6. How would you lead a nine- to 11-year-old to Christ as Savior?

Application Activities

1. Visit a day school class of nine- to 11-year-old children. Observe the students' actions and the teacher's methods of communication. Prepare a report of your findings.
2. Select a nine- to 11-year-old. Pray for him or her. Find out his/her interests and hobbies. Do something special with him/her. Help him/her understand spiritual truth from books, people, and experiences. Compare and discuss your findings.
3. Design a year's memory program for nine- to 11-year-olds. Select the verses and passages you want them to learn for each month. If possible, put your plan to work in a practical situation.

GROWING INDEPENDENCE

EARLY ADOLESCENCE

Ages 12, 13

7

There was a time in history when children went directly from childhood to adulthood. The culture was such that children began to assume adult roles shortly after they reached puberty.

David Bakan has argued that the invention or discovery of adolescence in America was largely in response to the social changes that accompanied America's development in the late nineteenth and early twentieth century. Bakan addresses three things that American society did to include adolescence as a period in the life cycle of a teen.

These three are: compulsory public education laws, child labor laws, and the juvenile justice system. The enactment of these laws resulted in adolescence becoming officially legislated as a period in the maturing person's life. [1]

Contrary to what some people believe, adolescence is not always a difficult transition period. For many it is a positive experience. Childhood activities give way to adolescent accomplishment which becomes adult achievement. Adolescents are seen standing between two worlds, that of childhood and adulthood. They try to act in adult ways and desire to be treated as an adult, yet they desire the security they experienced as children.

Adolescence includes three periods: early (ages 12,13), middle (ages 14-17), and later (ages 18-24), which is also considered beginning adulthood. Adolescence ends when adult maturity is evidenced physically, intellectually, emotionally, and socially.

The intensity of modern living often accelerates some aspects of maturity and sometimes results in abnormal adolescence. Poverty, misfortune, and sorrow may also affect this developmental period. Twelve or thirteen is often considered the beginning of adolescence. Girls enter into adolescent life earlier than boys which sometimes causes boy-girl and group relationship problems.

Developmental Tasks

Twelve- and 13-year-olds should achieve success in four developmental tasks—all essential to their successful progress through adolescence.

> Adjustment to rapidly changing bodies.
> Establishing a foundation for healthy adolescent independence.
> Achieving a sense of self-identity.
> Self-acceptance— appreciating and developing their strong traits, identifying and improving their weak areas.

Early Adolescence — *Complicated Change*

Persons between 12 and 13 are known as young adolescents, early youth, junior highs, early teens, or young teens. As in childhood, growth and development continues. Middle and later adolescence are also similar to childhood in that they are periods of adjustment and consolidation. Early adolescents' physical problems are complicated with changes in sexual functions. They see new powers awakening within them and adult aspirations stirring. This creates a turbulent mixture of tendencies and counter-tendencies. Complexities and contradictory traits are the natural order during these years.

Early adolescents are in a world of change and transition. Even though they don't understand themselves, they must not be misunderstood or ignored by others.

Twelve- and 13-year-olds need a special kind of adult with whom they can relate. The adults close to them must be loving, patient, and understanding. Those who work with young teens must use this unique opportunity to disciple them for Christ. Adults can do this if they:

> Keep channels of communication open.
> Multiply teens' interests.
> Guide by counsel and give direction.
> Provide companionship.

Often those working with youth can be the key to evangelism and Christian discipleship as they relate to teens during these years of religious awakening.

Physically — *Change*

The many physical changes taking place during early adolescence dramatically affect other major areas of adolescent development. The rate and degree of change is important.

Grow Rapidly and Unevenly

Early adolescents grow rapidly but unevenly. People at this age gain about twelve pounds a year and grow nearly six inches. This makes them feel self-conscious. The girls grow faster in early adolescence and are generally taller and heavier than boys during this period.

Their muscles seek strenuous activity. The sudden and conspicuous emergence of secondary sex characteristics makes young teens very conscious of their physical appearance. Most of them want either to gain or lose weight, would like to have better figures, and are seeking to improve their body build. They are often self-conscious about excessive features. [2]

The uneven growth rate of bones results in awkwardness. It confines adolescents and often frustrates and embarrrasses them. They need to be patient and understand that these changes are necessary as they leave childhood and gradually become adults.

Are Changing Internally

Puberty (when a person is first able to produce children) triggers development of the sex glands and is probably the most important change during these years. Girls develop sexually about one to two years ahead of boys. Because of these conditions young teens need sympathetic understanding and proper sex education.

Vital organs are growing rapidly. The heart nearly doubles, but it can easily be strained, developing heart murmurs. Lungs grow and glands become more active. Vocal cords almost double in length, making it hard for young teens to control their voice.

Growth Varies

Not only do the sexes develop at different rates but even among members of the same sex the development rate varies greatly. This phenomenon is sometimes called "early bloomers" or "late bloomers." Some late-maturing teens may not have experienced any change at all, while others, who are of the same age, have completed an entire stage of development.

Being a "late bloomer" can bring about a two-fold rejection—rejection by peers and self-rejection. Many teens may feel inadequate and may also be treated as incompetent. Therefore, for teens entering junior high the locker room may become a frightening experience.

Girls who are "early bloomers" may slouch in an attempt to compensate for their rapid growth. Boys may be given responsibility according to their size rather than their ability.

Experience Alternating Energy and Fatigue

Young teens' increasing strength is not always evenly distributed throughout their bodies. Spurts of energy alternate with fatigue. This protects the body against too much strain and is not mere laziness.

Both parents and others working with this age group must take into account that these young people need adequate rest. Therefore, all-night activities at retreats and camps could be unhealthy.

Intellectually — *Growing*

According to Piaget, adolescents are at the developmental stage where they are capable of serious thinking. They are developing their ability to grasp relationships and solve more complex problems. They grow in practical wisdom, in judgment, and common sense. Their knowledge grows faster than their experience, so those working with this age level must present problems for them to think through, direct them to the Scriptures to find answers, and then assist them in their search. [3]

Early adolescents have a new ability to deal with the abstract. They handle more symbolic ideas along with the concrete. They can memorize well, but must have a reason for it.

Those ministering to this age level can challenge capable 12- and 13-year-olds with resource materials and meaningful activities. They also can encourage slower learners and make them feel more secure and help them advance.

Young teens will not accept everything without questions. They want to know "why?" Why can't they go out with their friends at ten o'clock at night? When parents reject teens' requests without an appropriate answer, teens become highly critical. Because other adult leaders are authority figures like parents, teens have a tendency to be critical of them as well.

Young teens can be very critical. They insist that all things pass the test of their reasoning which is growing but is still limited by their lack of experience. Criticism in adolescence leads to conviction and individuality in adulthood. Every growing mind needs to seek understanding and wants proof. Doubts and questions are natural and healthy elements in intellectual growth.

Socially — *Seeking Companionship*

New attitudes shape early adolescents' social lives, especially their strong desire for peer group companionship. They want to be grown up and shun or feel superior to younger brothers and sisters. Their independence also makes them rebel and pull away from parents.

Seek Independence

Parents must recognize a natural growing independence. They must relinquish the reins more and more to young teens themselves. If they repress independence, they invite lasting weakness or constant friction, and ultimate lack of self-control. Teens often feel parents expect too much from them and don't really care.

Adults must learn to respect young teens' opinions and objections. Those ministering to youth and who are seeking to assume the role as their confidant, adviser, and counselor have a great opportunity since young teens are looking for significant adults outside the home.

Are Developing an Identity

Before adolescence, children learn a number of different roles such as student or friend, older brother, Christian, athlete, and so on. During adolescence, it is important to sort out and integrate these various roles into one consistent identity. Adolescents seek basic values and attitudes that cut across these various roles. If children fail to integrate a central identity or cannot resolve a major conflict between two major roles without opposing value systems, the result is what Erikson calls "ego diffusion." [4]

Therefore, achieving a sense of self-identity is crucial for adolescents. They begin to realize that all the pieces of themselves must fit into an integrated whole. They need the opportunity to talk things over, reflect on life around them and their own growing traits, potentials, and relationships. This is an important time for young people to find Christ as the central integrating factor for their lives.

Respond to Peer Pressure

Early adolescents are less secure as they move into new school experiences. Social contacts become more vital. Because of peer pressure, drugs can become a problem at this age.

Popularity is of supreme importance and the social pressure of their own age group is foremost. There is a naive desire for attention and prestige in the eyes of their peers, and a growing hunger for security. [5]

They want to have fun and do things with others and will be loyal to the group. Increased school activities, and possibly a part-time job, expand the peer group, making it more formidable than ever. Adults working with this age group should recognize this love and group organization and in it find potential for disciplined living, worthwhile activities, and choosing Christ as companion and leader.

Desire Special Friends

Usually young adolescent girls are more interested in the opposite sex than are boys. Although young teen boys are beginning to find girls attractive, they usually don't return this interest and girls may become involved with older boys. Early teens especially need close friends and confidants of their own sex.

Emotionally — *Fluctuation*

Emotional development parallels the physical. The emotions of young teens are quantitative more than qualitative, with quick, undefined shifts in emotional expression. With seemingly little reason, they bounce from joy to sorrow or agony to ecstasy. At times it appears that they lack emotional control. They may want to be with some people, but avoid others.

Most young teens are unstable, often over-responding—laughing or crying. "But you just don't understand!" is the frequent fiery exclamation of emotionally sensitive young teens as they retreat to their room and slam the door.

Sharing emotions can be a bewildering process to parents, who are often spectators. The whisperings, the secretiveness, the silence, the moodiness, and many other reflections of the inner life are difficult for adults to understand and to handle. [6]

Spiritually — *Challenge and Conversion*

Those ministering to this age level often underestimate the spiritual capacity of adolescents. Conversion really is a transformation, and in this particular period when change is the program of life, a spiritual transformation should be expected just as much as a physical change. It is the age of new beginnings.

Appreciate Personal Involvement

Adolescents' spiritual experiences are distinctly personal. They do not pray or attend church services simply because it is the custom. Personal conviction determines their decisions in these matters. Early teens need to realize that habits, even though formed in the preceding years, are a part of their individuality. Adult example is significant.

Moral dependence is decreasing. They express their own opinions and need more individual freedom of choice.

Regarding young teens' spiritual convictions, Soderholm says, young people at this age are not concerned with the philosophy of religion or the formulation of doctrines. They want a religion that works— one that will change their lives, satisfy their longings, and form their ideals. [7]

Need Moral Direction

According to Kohlberg, by the time children reach their teens most are at the level of conventional role conformity. That is, they are motivated to avoid punishment, are obedient-oriented, and are ready to abide by conventional moral stereotypes.

Adolescent values are, in part, a product of their experiences in making moral judgments. If individuals receive challenging, yet safe, opportunities to consider moral dilemmas at higher levels, adolescence may be a time of considerable moral development. [8]

Parents need to take the initiative for moral direction, but the church cannot stand idly by hoping that the parents will assume their roles. Seminars, films, discussion, and biblical principles must be shared with teens.

Experience Genuine Conversion

Early teens often are ready to accept Christ if challenged to do so by leaders they respect. A genuine conversion and open profession of faith in Christ at this time paves the way for continuing discipleship throughout adolescence. If not reached for Christ now, they may never be.

Develop Christian Character

Christian teens must be challenged to complete commitment and Christ-centered living. They are influenced by the example of Christian adults they respect. Adults who work with youth provide powerful role-models.

Early adolescents will have religious doubts but desire the stability which a firm foundation in the Word of God provides. They need assurance based on fact, not feelings. Those ministering to youth must discuss issues sympathetically and help them search for answers, patiently guiding them into the truth of God's Word.

Christian character is expressed in their desire to serve. Their energies and enthusiasm find satisfaction in meaningful Christian service.

Implications for Ministry

As young teens pass through this "in-between" stage, they should not be considered an anonymous "tween-ager." They should be accepted as people in their own right. Identity and self-acceptance are important issues, and the interest and program of the church should help them realize that the God who made them knows all about them, understands, and loves them.

A well-directed church youth group helps meet young teens' social as well as spiritual needs. Because they are important to the church, the Word becomes more important to them.

Because young teens want the privileges of adults, but not the responsibilities, those ministering to youth should stand before them as an example—beside them as a companion and friend—behind them as one who supports and encourages. This kind of leader will introduce them to the One who can live within them and enable them to say: "The Lord is the stronghold of my life; of whom shall I be afraid?" (Ps. 27:1b).

Young teens must be encouraged to study the Bible. Their readiness for learning, growing capacity for sustained attention, ability to discuss, and increased independence of thought make young teens challenging and responsive students of the Word. The church needs to help young teens understand the truth of James 3:17 and guide them toward attaining it, "the wisdom that comes from heaven is first of all pure; then peace-loving, considerate, submissive, full of mercy and good fruit, impartial and sincere."

Summary

Adolescence is an important transition period through which youth pass on their way from childhood to adulthood. It is a somewhat flexible period beginning with puberty in the early teens and terminating when adult maturity is achieved. It sometimes is divided into early, middle, and later adolescence.

Early adolescence is primarily a time of change, and physical development is the key to this period. Young teens need acceptance, understanding, and guidance. They are a challenge and need a challenge, for the foundation that is laid during the "childhood of adulthood" is vitally important to the adult years ahead. Those ministering to youth must be good adult examples, loving, understanding, and patient.

Notes
1. Daniel O. Aleshire, *Understanding Today's Youth* (Nashville: Convention Press, 1982), p. 26.
2. Roy G. Irving and Roy B. Zuck, eds., *Youth and the Church* (Chicago: Moody Press, 1968), p. 98.
3. Roy B. Zuck and Warren S. Benson, eds., *Youth Education in the Church* (Chicago: Moody Press, 1978), p. 120.
4. Grace Craig, *Human Development* (Englewood Cliffs, NJ: Prentice-Hall, Inc., 1983), pp. 46, 47.
5. Irving and Zuck, p. 101.
6. J. Edward Hakes, ed. *An Introduction to Evangelical Christian Education* (Chicago: Moody Press, 1964), p. 175.
7. Marjorie E. Soderholm, *Understanding the Pupil: Part III— The Adolescent* (Grand Rapids: Baker Book House, 1956), p. 31.
8. Craig, p. 374.

Discussion Questions
1. What are some significant differences between children and adults?
2. Name and identify the three periods of adolescence.
3. What principles should adults use in working with early teens?
4. How would you characterize the physical development of early teens?
5. List the highlights of the early teen's emotional and spiritual development.

Application Activities
1. Prepare a list of reasons why understanding early adolescents is basic to effectively ministering to them.
2. Interview several early teens for their advice to parents and other adult leaders. Compare answers and compile a report titled "Advice to Parents and Youth Workers."
3. Evaluate your church program for early teens in terms of meeting their needs. List strengths, weaknesses, and recommendations for improvement.

THE ACTION GENERATION

MIDDLE ADOLESCENCE

Ages 14-17

8

Fourteen- to 17-year-olds want to be where the action is. Their strong, maturing bodies; their alert and active minds; their strong but maturing emotions; their outgoing interest in others; their beginning philosophy of life; and their desire for a challenge—all combine to make middle adolescence an exciting time of life.

Developmental Tasks

No definite changes mark maturation from early to middle adolescence, but there are some distinguishing features. Middle adolescents now prepare for life's major responsibilities.

Havighurst lists the following as developmental tasks adolescents should achieve as they mature through adolescence to young adulthood:

> Achieving new and more mature relations with age-mates of both sexes.
>
> Achieving a masculine or feminine social role.
>
> Accepting one's physique and using the body effectively.
>
> Achieving emotional independence of parents and other adults.
>
> Achieving assurance of economic independence.
>
> Selecting and preparing for an occupation.
>
> Preparing for marriage and family life.
>
> Developing intellectual skills and concepts necessary for civic competence.
>
> Desiring and achieving socially responsible behavior.
>
> Acquiring a set of values and an ethical system as a guide to behavior. [1]

Physically — *Strengthened*
As mid-teens approach physical maturity, they realize personal responsibility and desire to achieve something for themselves. Their aspirations are not limited to the athletic field but often are reflected there.

Grow More Slowly
Although growth is slower, physical coordination is increasing. Boys gain in height and weight and usually catch up with the girls, who grow less after 16. Growth requires less energy. Boys can have tremendous appetites.

Mid-teens are stabilizing and forming both good and bad habits. They often experiment with tobacco, alcohol, and drugs as a result of bad adult examples, physical tastes, and peer pressure. They need to be reminded of the stewardship of their bodies (1 Tim. 5:22; 2 Tim. 2:20; Rom. 12:1,2).

Think About Appearance
Middle adolescent girls are concerned with looks and figures, while boys think of size and physical prowess. Both need to remember that physical appearance is only one aspect of total life development. Inner beauty and spiritual strength also are important (1 Sam. 16:7; 1 Pet. 3:3,4).

Need Good Hygiene Habits
For good physical development, adolescents need:
> Regular schedule, proper amount of sleep, proper diet, and exercise.
> Freedom from worry, which affects physical functions.
> A wholesome respect for themselves and others.
> Accurate knowledge of bodily changes and functions.
> Proper amount of responsible work activity.

Intellectually — *Alert*
Early adolescent criticism now develops into more promising judgment. They now experience an increasing place in society as their reasoning, self-control, independence, and outlook expand.

Achieve New Heights in Reasoning
The judgment of mid-teens is not yet mature, but their reasoning powers according to Piaget are developing rapidly and they are capable of thinking through complex problems. They ask why. They want reasons and reject easy authoritarian answers. These youth want to work with vital subject matter and need to get into and search the Word.

Their imagination is more creative and practical. It is often active in regard to future possibilities. In middle adolescence imagination reaches a high level and becomes the basis for idealistic dreams of great achievement. Learning how to live is as important as learning how to make a living.

Gain Independence and Responsibility

Success requires right habits along with knowledge. Mid-teens must become disciplined at home and school if they are to achieve self-control outside these settings. Many grow faster in independence than in self-discipline. The youths who are learning self-discipline faster than independence are becoming responsible. Until their training has led to self-conquest of body and mind, their education is unsuccessful. [2]

Seek Independence

Leaders must respect the individuality of middle adolescents so that intellectual power may develop. They should be encouraged to choose their vocation in line with distinct interests and abilities. Success comes if their heart, as well as hand and head, is in their chosen professions.

Middle adolescents enjoy forming their own opinions. They often know more concerning some subjects than their parents because of the knowledge explosion, their educational opportunities, and the mass media. As a result, they may develop a "know-it-all" attitude. They want to see the logic in everything and usually put together orderly arguments. They think and plan more logically and carry out longer-range plans. Special aptitudes are maturing. Vocational guidance needs to be given in a Christian setting.

Have Concern for Future

Middle adolescents' horizons broaden to include a world beyond themselves. They grow concerned about the future and are interested in those about them. They are subject to suggestions, with their peer group being most influential. They are also influenced by what they read, see, and hear in the media, as well as their actual experience.

Mid-teens are idealistic and creative. Their power to reason needs an outlet for expression. They assume responsibility but want and need guidance. Youth programs should channel this growing concern.

Socially — *Friendly*

As adolescents mature, social interests specialize. They need a smaller, more select group of friends. They, however, will still be friendly toward those outside their inner circle of friends. Maturing teens are out-going and interested in others.

Are Forming An Identity

Erikson believes that because the body is rapidly changing and because of the pressure by the family and society to make decisions about future education and career, teens need to question and redefine their identities that were established during earlier stages. [3]

Therefore, middle adolescence is an important period for identity formation. Teens prefer the company of friends to that of family. Family ties weaken and parent-teen relationships are often strained. As friends become more important to them, adolescents want reassurance that what they think about themselves is correct. Because of conflicting opinions from these friends, they must make the decision as to who they are as they observe their own self-image and what others think of that image. This can be devastating to their egos.

According to Zuck and Benson in *Youth Education in the Church,* however, Christian teens can be two or three steps ahead of their peers in forming their identities if they can accept what the Bible has to say about them, namely: that God designed them just as they are, that they are responsible to God, and that they have been redeemed by God through Jesus Christ. [4]

Desire Relationship with Opposite Sex

Socially, there almost always is a lively interest in the opposite sex. Each seeks admiration and companionship from the other. In many cases the relationships are rather superficial. Mid-teens generally are socially at ease and enjoy themselves.

The church's ministry to mid-teens should include helping them in boy-girl relationships and dating. Both church and home should help them adopt Christian standards and exercise the personal restraint needed for wholesome boy-girl relationships.

Are Interested in People

Interest in people seems to be a speciality for middle adolescents. They want friends, not just acquaintances, and usually have one or two close friends. They are influenced by successful adults. This interest in people is also expressed in involvement in meaningful service projects which enable them to see beyond themselves.

Emotionally — *Experienced*

The emotional life of middle adolescents is at a peak. They want to take every thrill and new experience while it lasts— an attitude that can be dangerous, physically and morally. Sometimes the results are reckless driving, drinking, drugs, improper sex.

Emotions are more qualitative, but still intense and fluctuating. Self-esteem and the desire to be considered adult are high priorities. These can be effective controlling factors with youth.

They hide feelings and may be secretive. They differentiate and enjoy varied experiences. Youth at this age like emotional reading and films and respond to emotional appeals. This has special significance in reaching them with the love of Christ.

Spiritually — *Real*

Spiritual interests fluctuate during middle adolescence, yet at this time many young people dedicate their lives to the Lord.

Respond to a Personal Faith

Christianity's personal aspect must be emphasized. Those ministering to this age level should show their faith by a personal relationship with Christ, rather than a list of do's and don'ts or by religious formality. Young people need the security and purpose of such a commitment to a personal God. Their Christian peers can best challenge them to commitment through personal witness and consistent living, but adults should also make every attempt to win unsaved teens to Christ.

Mid-teens are crusaders and respond to challenge and encouragement. They want active Christianity—an opportunity to be and to do. Aleshire, in *Understanding Today's Youth* says that youth should be challenged to think through the moral implications of their actions and behavior and be encouraged to consider the moral issues involved in the current events in their community and world.[5] Further, Irving and Zuck in *Youth and the Church* also stress that the importance of challenging youth to spiritual growth and service is reinforced by this fact: adult spiritual progress usually follows the trajectory established in mid-teens.[6] Young people must not become spiritually complacent.

Prefer Religious Experience

The inner religious experience of 14- to 17-year-olds is closely related to sentiment and social implications. They need to ally their spiritual experience with life decisions. The actions of the group will have a strong influence if they don't have their own standards. Like Daniel, they can purpose not to defile themselves (Dan. 1:8). Their spiritual growth often comes in big strides.

Youth need consistent and committed leadership. This type of leadership does not dominate but guides. It allows young people to take responsibility for their own spiritual decisions.

Doubt Faith

Strong inner desires run counter to Christian direction. Inconsistent adults trouble teens—especially if they are parents, youth workers, or other Christian leaders. Teens can be further confused by contradictory objectives of different agencies contacting youth. School teachings may contradict the Bible. A lack of spiritual reality may produce doubts. Earlier questions may not have been answered adequately. Or faith may have been based on feelings rather than the Word of God.

Parents and other adults ministering to youth must listen to young people when they express doubts. Their experience encourages them to question, search, and examine the evidence. This questioning approach should be treated with respect, so it can be used to teach the reality of Christ.

Appreciate Worship

Spiritual openness, appreciation of reverence, and worship can be real steps toward worshipping in spirit and in truth (John 4:24). Young people need to be taught to "worship the Lord in the beauty of holiness" (Ps. 96:9). They need to experience God in His majesty, greatness, and power.

As young people learn that "the fear of the Lord is the beginning of wisdom" (Prov. 9:10) and the "fear of the Lord is to hate evil" (Prov. 8:13), they are on the way to meaningful worship.

Implications for Ministry

The total church program for youth should be one of action, balance, and purpose to meet youth's quest for meaning and purpose in life. Questions youth ask should be handled honestly. When answers are not known, those ministering to youth should admit it and search with young people for the truth.

Middle adolescents need to be trained and given responsibility—opportunity for achievement and service. "Use me or lose me" is still their cry. They can be involved in important projects, not just busy work. "Flee the evil desires of youth, and pursue righteousness, faith, love, and peace, along with those who call on the Lord out of a pure heart" (2 Tim. 2:22) is relevant counsel for teens today.

Those who minister to 14- to 17-year-olds must be able to identify with, love, and appreciate them. Their lives must be well-balanced and exemplary as they guide, counsel, and instruct.

The youth program of the church must challenge them for God and true discipleship. Scriptural standards learned at home and church can give meaning and stability to teenage life.

Summary

Middle adolescents are part of the "action generation." Here's where the action is! Physically middle teens are on the move toward maturity. They want to achieve in many areas. They are learning more than ever and are quite sophisticated. They strongly desire independence and freedom but are not fully prepared for all the reality and responsibility that it brings. They move in the circle and influence of the peer group, with a lively interest in the opposite sex. They desire quality and depth of emotional experience, crave thrills, and new experiences. They are interested in spiritual things. Middle adolescents are a challenge and demand a challenge.

Notes

1. R. J. Havighurst, *Human Development and Education* (New York: David McKay Co., 1953), pp. 111-58.
2. Roy B. Zuck and Warren S. Benson, eds., *Youth Education in the Church* (Chicago: Moody Press, 1978), p. 133.
3. Robert E. Slavin, *Educational Psychology* (Englewood Cliffs, NJ: Prentice-Hall, 1988), p. 40.
4. Zuck and Benson, p. 134.

5. Daniel O. Aleshire, *Understanding Today's Youth* (Nashville: Convention Press, 1982), p. 139.
6. Roy G. Irving and Roy B. Zuck, eds., *Youth and the Church* (Chicago: Moody Press, 1968), p. 116.

Discussion Questions

1. What are some ways a teenager can attain good physical development?
2. Why are reasoning, self-control, independence, and expanded outlook necessary for teens?
3. What are the main areas of social significance for the middle teen?
4. Briefly characterize the middle adolescent emotionally.
5. Show how experience is important to spiritual development in middle adolescence.

Application Activities

1. Observe a middle adolescent with whom you are acquainted. Note characteristics in the five main areas of development as well as special interests and needs. Write a report and compare findings.
2. Evaluate your church program for senior high young people in terms of challenging them and meeting their needs. List strengths, weaknesses, and recommendations.
3. Interview some teens with these questions:
   What do you do that makes your faith personal?
   Have you ever doubted your faith? If so, what caused it?
   How have you expressed your faith to others?
   What type of worship service do you like best? Why?
   Discuss what you learn from their answers.

PERIOD OF TRANSITION

BEGINNING ADULTHOOD

Ages 18-24

9

Adulthood covers a wide span of years with people spending more time as an adult than in any other developmental stage. The range of years triples that of all previous age groups.

According to Craig, the term "adult" usually refers to being grown-up, full-size, or mature. "A vast array of psychological characteristics usually associated with maturity are: psychological independence and autonomy, independent decision making, and some degree of stability, wisdom, reliability, integrity, and compassion. Different investigators put different characteristics into the blend, and different cultures demand different sets of responsibilities." [1]

The great age range within the adult years calls for subdivisions. Most people agree on at least three major periods: beginning or young adults, middle adults, and later or older adults. Few agree about the dividing lines, for it is impossible to pinpoint the particular time one passes from level to level in adulthood. This study will consider young adulthood in two parts. The first part is labeled "beginning adulthood" (ages 18-24) and the last part, considered in the next chapter is titled "young adulthood" (ages 25-34).

Beginning Adulthood

Moore labels this age level as a period of transition. He points out that it is the years between middle adolescence and adulthood and can be characterized by decision-making. Such issues as self-support, life occupation, friends, marriage, abortion, drugs, war, ecology, and the world confront beginning adults. [2] Furthermore, young adults at this time in their lives are asking themselves such questions as "Who am I?," "How do I relate to others?," and "What should I believe?" Their ques-

71

tions concern identity, interrelationships, and ideology.

In considering this age group it is best to keep in mind that it includes college students, employed persons, married couples, and those who still live with their parents, by themselves, or with a friend.

Developmental Tasks

Considering adulthood to begin at age 18, Havighurst states that during this period, young adults face eight developmental tasks. These tasks serve as signs of development, or measures of progress, through this stage of adult experience.

The eight developmental tasks are:

Selecting a mate (or adjusting to unmarried adult status).

Learning to live with a marriage partner.

Starting a family.

Rearing children (or learning to relate to children of others).

Managing a home.

Getting started in an occupation.

Taking on civic responsibilities.

Finding a congenial social group. [3]

Added to these should be establishing or continuing a right relationship with God.

Physically — *Biological Prime*

In the years between 18 and 24, men and women are reaching a peak of vitality, strength, and endurance. Young adults generally enjoy better health than do children. They are in their biological prime. The rate of death for this age group is lower than most other groups.

Recruiting young men and women to do battle, huge sums of money paid to athletes, students facing exhausting studies and internships, bar exams, exhausting manual labor, and young women expected to give birth, is how most cultures recognize the physical prime. [4]

Beginning adults have a great abundance of energy to dedicate to the Lord's work. Since young adults may not have established themselves in a career or gotten married, they often are more available for short-term missionary service. Being only a few years older than the teenagers in the local church, they often can identify with this age level and work effectively with them in Sunday school, camp, and/or club work.

Intellectually — *Formal Operations*

Jean Piaget suggested four basic stages in intellectual behavior. The fourth is "formal operations." At this stage in life, beginning adults are able to handle symbolism and abstract ideas. They can explore the logical solutions to a problem, can imagine things contrary to fact, and can think realistically about the future and form ideals. If thinking is too abstract or theoretical, however, beginning adults may revert to concrete reasoning because they feel more comfortable at that level.

Develop Reasoning Capacity

The cognitive development of beginning adults is very important because it is during this period that intellectually they are solving problems and making many decisions. This reasoning capacity helps the young adult in pursuing a career and choosing the proper lifestyle. Therefore, this period by some may be called an "achieving period."

Begin to Accept Others' Opinions

Craig further points out that "Confronted with differences of opinion, uncertainty, and confusion, the young adult begins to accept, or even respect a diversity of opinion. They begin to adopt the point of view that different people have the right to different opinions, and even understand that one person can see the same thing in two different ways depending on the particular context." [5]

Have Intellectual Doubts

Intellectually doubting one's faith is normal and should be considered as part of the maturation process. As children and teens pass through various intellectual stages in their thinking process, however, parents and church leaders need to help them develop their intellectual knowledge regarding the faith. In this way, young adults discover the answers to the question, "What should I believe?"

Emotionally — *Advancing Toward Stability*

Beginning adults are better able to control their emotions, therefore, they tend to avoid making decisions on emotion alone. Thus they need to be approached from reason even when making spiritual decisions.

Possess Fear of Worry

Although they no longer have childhood fears, beginning adults possess the fear of worry. They may worry about their relationship with the opposite sex, job security, schooling, and the future regarding the will of God for their lives. One way they may compensate for these worries is by overeating or not eating at all.

Face Loneliness

Many times single adults face loneliness because they have difficulty relating to their peers. They are tempted by immorality as they strive to satisfy their emotional needs. They want to be free of any commitments and responsibility, yet they want the intimacy of a significant relationship.

Socially — *Independent*

Social feelings strengthen, develop, and broaden, as new and lasting friendships can be established during college and early career years. Although beginning adults seek to break away from the family while seeking to find their identity, they want the security of the home.

Think Independently

Beginning adults are learning to think independently and no longer accept the ideas of the majority. They enjoy informal discussions regarding the issues of the day. They accept those who agree with them and like to argue with those who do not. They enjoy taking the place of leadership in various organizations.

Are Establishing Significant Relationships

According to Craig, "In beginning adulthood, the central developmental conflict is that of intimacy versus isolation. The intimacy that Erikson talks about concerns more than sexual intimacy. It is an ability to share one's self with another person of either sex without fear of losing one's own identity." [6]

Face Severe Problems

The transition from adolescence to adulthood is often accompanied by severe problems. One writer suggestions the following: divorce, suicide, college dropout, sexual problems, crime, and problems of general disorganization of many young adults—inability to attach or adjust to society and a tendency to rulelessness. "The use of drugs among some young adults is more related to this general psychological state than to any other reason." [7]

Beginning adults can easily drift away from the church. Yet, at no other time in life is a right relationship with God more needed than in the period when persons are developing their philosophy of life, choosing life partners, and life's work.

Spiritually — *Growing*

Early in this period, beginning adults question their faith and beliefs. Questions are normal and young adults will not lose their faith just because they are demanding a reason for it.

Are Asking About Their Beliefs

"What should I believe?" is the question young adults are asking as they seek to form a philosophy of life. Until young adults can answer this question they lack the sorting mechanism through which they can pass their impressions of life. The college campus and the world of work often present many contrary views of life that may challenge students who are not well grounded in God's Word.

Need Guidance on Spiritual Gifts and God's Will

Many beginning adults are unaware of what their spiritual gifts are or what God's will is for their lives. Many feel their busy schedules prevent them from studying the Bible and praying daily. Feeling this way, however, cuts them off from the main source for discovering God's will. Even though they may have the gift of evangelism, they may not be able to share their faith because they lack confidence or ability or may feel they have no nonbelieving friends.

May Consider the Church Irrelevant

Some beginning adults consider the church irrelevant, not because God is irrelevant nor because they are resistant to the faith, but for some, it is because "adult" Christians are playing church rather than living a consistent and victorious Christian life. Others have considered the biblical message irrelevant on the basis that the church does not see their problems from their viewpoint.

Seek Answers Church Can Provide

One study done among members of this group said that even though new responsibilities and interests may be distracting, beginning adults are very much in need of what Christ and the church have to offer them. Breaking home ties presents the need for new friends. New work experiences reveal to them their limitations. Family responsibilities shake their previous self-confidence. Beginning adults are usually open and grateful for any help that will enable them to find answers to their problems.[8]

Implications for Ministry

It is imperative to reach unchurched (non-Christian) beginning adults for Christ. He is the only one who can provide true meaning and purpose to life. He gives courage and wisdom.

At church, beginning adults should meet Christ as Savior, make close friends, choose a life partner, and find help in determining a life vocation. Here they can find fulfilling service opportunities.

A vital ministry to beginning adults is a challenge. It must begin by meeting them where they are— in the midst of their needs. The key to this ministry is often the dynamic, personable, spiritual leaders.

Spiritual reproduction is important in this period. The kind of spiritual heritage (or lack of it) beginning adults provide for their children will affect the next generation. Beginning adults who remain single also can effectively influence children and youth for God. Members of this age should be taught principles of evangelism and witness through service. Learning to disciple others is also important.

The church can reach out to beginning adults through the infant and toddler ministry, friendship evangelism, home Bible study classes, as well as the church's program of instruction, worship, fellowship, and service. Elective subjects in the church educational program can meet needs such as family instruction, worship, and fellowship.

Concerned pastors should include marriage counseling and home building as a part of their ministries. When the church provides an effective ministry to beginning adults, they will remain loyal to Christ and will be good parents to their children.

Summary

Beginning adulthood (18-24) is a period of transition as the young adult faces such developmental tasks as preparing for and starting an occupation, selecting a mate, and having children.

Physically, young adults are in their prime. Intellectually, they have the ability to solve problems and make many decisions. Intellectually questioning their faith is normal and is part of the growing process. Although they are emotionally stable, they worry about their relationships with the opposite sex, schooling, and the future. Socially, they are becoming more independent as they move away from home. During this period they are assuming various leadership roles on the college campus and in the church. Their greatest role may be that of developing a significant relationship in marriage. Spiritually, they are growing as they claim ownership of their faith. Sometimes they lack the knowledge of what their spiritual gifts are and what God's will is for their lives. The church and the biblical message have sometimes become irrelevant for beginning adults. An important ministry to beginning adults in the church is essential to the on-going life and ministry of the church.

Notes

1. Grace Craig, *Human Development* (Englewood Cliffs, NJ: Prentice-Hall, 1989), p. 424.
2. Allen J. Moore, *The Young Adult Generation* (Nashville: Abington Press, 1969), pp. 125-127.
3. R. J. Havighurst, *Human Development and Education* (New York: David McKay Co., 1953), p. 2.
4. Craig, p. 428.
5. Craig, p. 433.
6. Craig, p. 47.
7. Moore, pp. 146,147.
8. *The Age Group Objectives of Christian Education,* The Boards of Parish Education of four Lutheran Churches (Philadelphia: W. Kent Gilbert, 1958), p. 88.

Discussion Questions

1. How would you describe the beginning adult physically, intellectually, emotionally, socially, and spiritually— in ten words or less.
2. Discuss the challenge of meeting the needs of beginning adults socially and how the church can meet those needs.
3. Why is this period often a time of emotional stress and strain?
4. List and explain the spiritual dilemmas that beginning adults face.
5. What can the church do to help beginning adults feel the church is still relevant to their lives?

Application Activities

1. Discuss the spiritual shortcomings that young adults face and determine how the church can meet each of these.
2. Interview several church leaders in your church and other local churches to determine what the church should be doing to minister to young adults on a continuing basis.
3. How can the church minister to the wide variety of young adults in your community?

DECADE OF DEVELOPMENT

YOUNG ADULTHOOD

Ages 25-34

10

Having begun adulthood during the transition years of higher education and/or beginning a career, young adults continue the maturation process during the next decade of development and growth. The early years, according to Moore, involve "...a cluster of crises which must be resolved if one is to move with any semblance of adequacy into adulthood."[1] Even if some of these crises are not difficult to negotiate, it is still necessary to walk along life's normal path pressing on to maturity.

Beginning adulthood, as presented in the last chapter, is similar to Levinson's "Early Adult Transition" period, 17-22 years. He divides young adulthood into: "Entering the Adult World" (23-28); "Age 30 Transition" (28-33); and "Settling Down" (33-40).[2] This chapter is concerned with ages 25-34.

Developmental Tasks

Havighurst's developmental tasks for young adults were given in the previous chapter. Here it may be helpful to note that the central developmental stage of young adulthood in Erikson's ages and stages of the life cycle is "intimacy or isolation." Intimacy relates to the ability to risk one's self in relations of closeness with others. The opposite tendency is isolation. The virtue or strength that emerges in a balance toward intimacy is that of love.[3]

Physically — *A Peak*

The young adult's body achieves its final development integration in the early years of this period, reaching its full skeletal and muscular development between ages 20 and 30. Coordination, mastery, and maturity are evident.

Attain Ultimate Body Strength

The peak period of striped (voluntary) muscle strength is usually reached between the ages of 25 and 30. "Physical strength is at its maximum between ages 15 and 30; after 30 it declines slowly but significantly. Despite signs of aging, most physical skills and capacities remain at a functional level if regularly exercised." [4] Physical endurance reaches a peak along with the specialization of skills. Speed of response and ability to learn new motor skills are at maximum levels by the mid-twenties. In the midst of a busy, expanding world, 25- to 34-year olds' physical powers are at their best. Near the end of the period, however, physical fitness may begin to decline. The rate of decline can be slowed by persistent efforts to keep in good health and physical condition through proper diet, regular exercise, and good health habits.

Enjoy Good Health

Most young adults enjoy good health. They have yet to experience the physical problems of middle age. Most major athletes reach their prime during this period. The physical job skills needed by young adults are at maximum efficiency. It should be noted, however, that "although no symptoms may be felt, many signs of disease that will cause trouble in later life, such as heart, lung, and kidney disease, joint and bone problems, atherosclerosis, cirrhosis of the liver, are beginning to develop." [5]

Tend to Overdo

The pressure of the daily routine at home and at work is continuous and quite heavy. Many times men at this age will over-exert themselves physically to get established vocationally and financially. Health problems as well as home problems could result from spending too much time away from the family.

Establishing a home and perhaps starting a family coupled with their abundant energy often awakens or renews interest in the Lord's work. Young adult fellowship groups and/or a variety of local church activities for young children often rise in importance. Young adults should avoid the barrenness of a busy life. Too much work, even the Lord's work, together with an emphasis on making a living often leads to stress related problems.

Intellectually — *Full Capacity*

Young adults continue to be very capable of new learning. They are idealistic, independent, adventuresome. Life now takes on a new reality, however, as some romantic dreams fade.

Develop Reasoning Capacity

This age has fully developed reasoning capacities. Reason is more in line with personal convictions. Their general interests and learning interests are more specialized—focused on a life work.

Recognize Others' Opinions

Young adults are interested in what others think. They gear in on the place of history and established authorities. Some may emphasize present experience and disdain traditions, challenging authority.

Continue Resolving Doubts

Intellectual doubts may carry over from unresolved early adulthood and adolescent doubts. At this age, it becomes evident that a faith proven at each age level is a faith fortified against doubt and skepticism.

Jesus said, "Learn from me" (Matt. 11:29a). Christianity can challenge young adults' keen learning ability. They need to see faith as a reasoning faith, dig into the Word of God for themselves, and then learn to share their faith with others.

Emotionally — *Advance in Stability*

Continued emotional maturity throughout this period is essential to true adulthood. The deeper and finer emotions are strengthened or weakened. Moderation marks young adults who have become well-rounded, independent persons.

Young people tend to enter adulthood optimistically and full of expectation. Then gradually life is reorganized as the struggle continues between dreams and reality, idealism and experience. Idealism is being tempered by reality and experience.

Emotional turmoil can easily break through these happy, exciting years with frustration and disappointment accompanying adjustments. Loneliness and many temptations face single adults as they strive to satisfy their emotional needs. Nor are the married young adults without problems as they must learn many new roles.

Happy are single young adults who become adequate people. Then if married, the adequate person becomes an adequate partner and parent. They do not carry unsolved emotional problems into this period of life from adolescence. They can develop emotional maturity and successfully evaluate themselves, their life-styles, and experiences with a view toward improving the quality of their lives.

Socially — *Family Centered*

Social feelings strengthen and develop as new and lasting friendships established during the college and early career years are continued into adulthood and perhaps young married life. Social life revolves around key friends, the home, informal and organized groups.

Some young adults are postponing marriage until the later twenties and early thirties. When married, they concentrate on the family and home interests. They must adjust to interpersonal relationships with a marriage partner, parents, children, and in-laws.

"The church's ministry of discipling finds a natural base in the home and family," writes Charles Sell, "where children and adults alike should be nurtured, grow, and mature. Being Christian in the home is as imperative for the Christian as it is challenging (Deut. 6:1-9; Eph. 5:22-6:4; Col. 3:18-24). In today's troubled homes, it is not always easy to incorporate scriptural precepts into life behind the front door. The church should encourage personal maturity by fostering family growth, because individual stages are intricately interwoven with family stages." [6]

These can be lonely years for single young adults, who are struggling to free themselves from their families and establish meaningful friendships in a marriage-oriented society. Single adults often become much involved in group work and social concerns. Tying them to home responsibilities limits their social life-style.

Adjustments also must be made in the vocational life. Problems often arise regarding relationships with associates and work can demand so much time that home and social life is harmed.

Spiritually — *Building Foundations*

Early in this period, young adults reevaluate religious thoughts and beliefs. This serves a good purpose, for spiritually these are foundational years, leading to successful living as an adult.

The reality of adulthood together with its pressures demand a growing, dynamic faith. Unless faith is deepened during these years and loyalty to Christ and His church is renewed, spiritual concerns will be overshadowed and crowded out.

Adults at this age sometimes tend toward materialism. The desire for money and the quest for temporal things can grow unchecked. The Master's reminder is needed: "Watch out! Be on your guard against all kinds of greed; a man's life does not consist in the abundance of his possessions" (Luke 12:15). Young adults must remember that God is supreme and preeminent, and to do all to His glory (1 Cor. 10:31).

Activity and busyness can militate against the things of the spirit. In the years of preparing for a career and in making a living, young adults must remember that they are building a life as well.

Implications for Ministry

Evangelism continues to be important throughout the adult years. Reaching young adults for Christ must continue to be a priority.

Once establishing a personal relationship with Christ, young adults must catch a vision of the Lord's requirements for them. Lois LeBar outlined what the Lord expects of them this way:

> constantly maturing in their personal lives,
> maintaining a joyous Christian home,
> developing and using their spiritual gifts,
> doing a bang-up job in one responsibility in the church,
> reflecting Christ in their vocations,
> evangelizing the natural contacts they make outside the church,
> and taking their part in community affairs. [7]

This applies to all adult ages, but certainly must be a vision of those in the latter part of young adulthood.

When people visualize themselves meeting these expectations, they certainly will be more aware of their needs. The church's continuing education and equipping ministry should be active in helping meet these needs, and thus be equipping the saints for the work of service, and be building up the body of Christ (Eph. 4:12).

Summary

The range of the adult years challenges church ministry. The term "adult" assumes full growth physically with continuing growth in other areas—intellectually, emotionally, socially, spiritually.

Physically people 25-34 years old are equipped to take the strain and stress needed in getting established as an adult. Some young adults are still making important choices—life's partner and work. Vocationally young adults are getting established. For those who are married, social interests center in the home and family. A Christ-centered philosophy of life is imperative. Spiritually these are important foundational years for living successfully as an adult.

Notes

1. Allen J. Moore, *The Young Adult Generation* (Nashville: Abington Press, 1969), pp. 125-27.
2. Daniel J. Levinson, et. al., *The Seasons of a Man's Life* (New York: Knopf, 1978), p. 57.
3. Erikson, Erik, *Identity and the Life-Cycle: A Reissue* (New York: Norton, 1980), pp. 51-107.
4. Grace Craig, *Human Development*, 5th ed. (Englewood Cliffs, NJ: Prentice-Hall, 1989). p. 428.
5. Craig, p. 429.
6. Charles M. Sell, *Transition* (Chicago: Moody Press, 1985), pp. 53, 54.
7. Lois E. LeBar, *Focus on People in Church Education* (Westwood, NJ: Fleming H. Revell Co., 1968), pp. 183,184.

Discussion Questions

1. Using one word for each characteristic, describe the young adult physically, intellectually, emotionally, socially, and spiritually.
2. What affects the emotional development of young adults?
3. How can the church best help young adults in preparing for Christian marriage and establishing a Christ-centered home?
4. What can the church do to reach young adults for Christ?
5. How would you characterize the social life of young adults with whom you are acquainted?

Application Activities

1. Determine a program a church can use to prepare young adults for Christian marriage and the establishment of a home.
2. With widely varied educational backgrounds, how can the church reach all young adults in its community?
3. Prepare a church social program which will meet the needs of young adults.

POWER OF THE COMMUNITY

MIDDLE ADULTHOOD

Ages 35-64

11

In many ways, middle age is more a state of mind than a span of years. The years from 35-64 are chosen more for their social and psychological factors than chronological. Most developmental tasks of young adulthood are completed by the early thirties. Middle adulthood becomes a period of continuing, developing, maturing, and deepening.

After discovering an expanding world in young adulthood, middle adults find expansiveness curtailed and move toward deepening and strengthening relationships and experiences. Middle adults need to integrate their entire personalities around Christ for the Christian finds strength and depth in the Christ-centered, spirit-controlled life.

The concepts of "generativity versus stagnation," according to Erikson, characterize the main challenge middle adults face. The generative person has a grown-up identity. When generativity overcomes (or balances) stagnation, person's lives show the strength or virtue of care. [1]

The five characteristics of this period are: achievement, establishment, responsibility, evaluation, and adjustment.

During middle age a person should have a capacity for maximum vocational achievement. Family adjustments and readjustments should come quickly. Havighurst says of middle adults, "With an increased understanding of the stewardship of the totality of life, men and women can discover a creative usefulness in church, home, and community—finding deeper and deeper meanings and satisfactions in living." [2]

Developmental Tasks

During middle adulthood, the following tasks are expected to be achieved:

Achieving adult civic and social responsibility.

Establishing and maintaining an economic standard of living.

Assisting teen-age children to become responsible and happy adults.

Developing adult leisure-time activities.

Relating to one's spouse as a person.

Accepting and adjusting to the physiological changes of middle age.

Adjusting to aging parents. [3]

To these a spiritual dimension might be added: establishing or continuing a right relationship with God.

Physically — *Beginning Decline*

Middle age adults are past the height of physical efficiency. During these years of life, although they experience a gradual reduction of the body's capacity to function and perform, it has relatively little impact on their typical daily activities. With increasing age and conditions of stress, however, the impact might be greater.

Experience Some Limitations

After 45, ailments may begin to develop and organic weaknesses may appear. Arthritis, high blood pressure, and digestive disturbances may increase. Lessened auditory and visual acuity may also become more noticeable after age 55. Although wide individual differences are possible, about a 10 percent loss in muscle strength usually occurs between ages 30 to 60.

Have Changing Sex Drives

Physiological changes affect the sex drive. Sexual power and ability may decline. During menopause, in the forties or early fifties, women lose their reproductive function. Men's decline in sexual power and desire is slower but does not affect their reproductive ability.

Accept Physical Change

Physical changes can cause concern. It is important for middle age adults to adjust realistically for successful living. Men may go beyond their capacities, or physical condition, to prove they can still compete with younger men. Middle adult women, concerned with physical appearance, want to keep looking youthful but should accept limitations. Menopause can be a problem for some women, but for many the physical and emotional changes of menopause are minimal. A wholesome Christian perspective can help greatly in accepting physical changes.

Perform Valuable Service

While middle adults are limiting physical activity, they often find new opportunities in places of church leadership, which utilizes their experience and maturity in teaching, planning, and supervising. Steward-ship of the body as the temple of the Holy Spirit is increasingly important for keeping the same pace as in earlier years may en-danger health.

Intellectually — *Productive and Persistent*

Middle adults find their mental powers and skills productive and challenging. Judgment is sound and dependable. There is wider per-spective with practical application. Reason is dominant, sometimes tending toward inflexibility, quiet persistence, conservativism, and a matter-of-fact approach.

Middle adults often experience a slight decrease in the rate of their learning, but with more purposefulness, self-confidence, and a feeling of competence, they can often overcome any decrease. Those who are mentally alert experience wide knowledge and for many this period is one of great achievement in mental tasks.

Since age has little affect on the capacity for learning, adults should be encouraged to continue to learn. Many-faceted adult education pro-grams provide opportunities for this.

In this period of achievement and wide learning opportunity, there is a tendency to specialize. Specialization overemphasized sometimes causes middle adults to lose the intellectual breadth increased exper-ience otherwise gives.

Carry Burdens

The burdens of life tend to multiply in middle age. One writer points out that if people are unsuccessful by the time they reach forty, the bur-den of their failure rests heavily upon them and the chances of sur-mounting their difficulty and overcoming their defeat become increas-ingly remote. On the other hand, if they are successful by forty, respon-sibility rests heavily on their shoulders as the load grows heavier from year to year. [4]

Emotionally — *Deep and Full*

Middle age often is the period of burden bearing. Yet, middle adults may find these years the most satisfying of adulthood. They tend to be realistic and practical. It is a time of self-control—with emotions run-ning deep and full. Personal reverses may bring bitterness and dis-illusionment, however, which may be hard to overcome.

Emotional maturity often continues although increasing age does not guarantee emotional growth. Fixed attitudes may develop and retard such growth. Resistance to change is likely to interfere with the maturing of values, interests, and concepts. Often middle adults refuse to match their outlooks with life's new horizons. For the Christian, the fruit of the Spirit (Gal. 5:22,23) is essential to emotional and spiritual maturity.

For some, especially men, this is a time of crisis. Craig reports that men in mid-life crisis are confused and feel that their whole world is disintegrating. They are unable to meet demands and solve problems. For some men, this may be a temporary phase; for others, it may be the beginning of a continuous decline. [5]

How one feels about physical changes is almost as important as the changes themselves. Though middle adults may try to hide signs of growing older, they can adjust to decreasing physical abilities and find satisfaction and happiness in other areas of activity. Quality of work and experience now receive new emphasis.

They have many opportunities to help teenagers become mature Christian adults. Emotionally, this can produce great joy and encourage emotional stability and maturity among parents and leaders.

Socially — *Renewed Interest*

Middle adults are often building and maintaining happy family relationships as parents or grandparents while maintaining a circle of friends outside the family.

Relate to Groups

Much time and energy is spent gaining social position in the community. Middle-aged adults are "belongers"—with a variety of organizations claiming their attention, time, and money. They often occupy responsible and authoritative positions in society and administer and control its various institutions.

Adjust to Smaller Family

Loneliness and concern may develop as children leave the home. Parents may have considered the children a burden when they were young, but a sense of concern grips them as they see them reach maturity, leave the home nest, and go into the world for themselves.

Husband and wife learn to live alone again, especially if they tended to neglect each other while the children were at home. They may even have to learn to love again as, in a new way, they focus on each other as persons.

Middle-aged adults may find themselves involved in helping their children become established, giving increased attention to aging parents, and striving to prepare for their own retirement, all at the same time. Often they face the death of a parent or even a spouse and are forced to make unwelcome adjustments in life.

Face Marriage Problems

This can be a dangerous period for marriages. In the later years of middle age, established family patterns are often broken by divorce and remarriage. Even people who may have seemed comfortable with their relationship sometimes overturn everything for what seems to be a newer, more exciting change. This problem is increased by the lowering moral standards in society at large and the pressure to conform.

Need Fellowship

Many middle adults' social needs can be met through well-balanced fellowship programs. Churches must emphasize deep fellowship—true *koinonia,* as the New Testament speaks of it. This kind of fellowship grows into effective outreach. The church can reach middle-aged adults for Christ through its members witnessing through word and deed in the neighborhood, community, and marketplace. A helping hand to those who are on the move or new in the community is always welcome. Caring and sharing opportunities abound.

Spiritually — *Burden Bearing*

Christian middle-aged adults sense spiritual realities and need to integrate their entire personality around Christ. He is the only one who can give strength for a life of power, poise, and accomplishment.

Since middle adults have a dominant place in the life of the church and home, the effectiveness of the church's ministry to the young depends much upon what is being done with and by adults.

Middle adults must remember that the degree of outward success they attain is not an accurate measure of their success in fulfilling the will of God. Along with success in daily work, Christians need to continually remember that all life is sacred and to be lived in the will of God. Adults' spiritual needs can be met during this tri-decade through a balanced church program. Evangelism is important. Reaching adults becomes the key for reaching homes and families for Christ and the church.

Serve Willingly

Middle adults are interested in practical expression and service activities. Since they invest their time, effort, and money in many good causes, they should be enlisted fully in the best cause—for Christ. Such involvement, however, must not come at the expense of proper family life. The church must supplement the home, not supplant it.

Implications for Ministry

The church's ministry to adults must be realistic—meeting people where they are, helping them meet and solve middle-aged problems with divine resources. It should evidence the kind of spiritual vitality which will aid adults to realize the abundant life Christ came to give (John 10:10)—purpose, power, poise, peace, and a sense of accomplishment (2 Tim. 1:7). A church must not just use middle adults—it must minister to them as well.

The church's educational program should—through systematic study of the Bible—help adults become better equipped for Christian living and service. Elective study courses add new dimension to adult learning in the church.

Effective ministry must still focus on the home, business, and social needs of adults. As most of the activities of the home and church are planned and supervised by adults, they play a dominant role in guiding and leading the various ministries of the church during these years.

Summary

Many believe middle age is the best time of life. It can be a wonderful period for the Christian. Though declining some physically, middle adults generally enjoy good health and are in good physical condition if they give proper care to their bodies. They are mentally productive with abilities and skills at their best. Learning is still an adventure. Socially, middle adults find renewed interest. The emotions run deep and full. In these areas of life, middle age should demonstrate true maturity. A well-balanced ministry to adults in the church will help to successfully meet the spiritual needs of middle age. This is important because middle-aged adults are bearing the burden of two very important institutions— the church and the home.

Notes

1. Erik H. Erikson, *Identity and the Life Cycle* (New York: International Universities Press, 1959), pp. 95-99. Reissue (New York: Norton, 1980), pp. 51-107.
2. R. J. Havighurst, *Human Development and Education* (New York: David McKay Co., 1953), p. 49.
3. Havighurst, pp. 268-76.
4. Gaines S. Dobbins, *Teaching Adults in the Sunday School* (Nashville: Convention Press, 1936), pp. 29,30
5. Grace Craig, *Human Development*, 5th ed. (Englewood Cliffs, NJ: Prentice-Hall, 1989), pp. 528,529.

Discussion Questions

1. What developmental tasks do middle adults need to attain?
2. What difference can a wholesome Christian perspective make in accepting physical changes?
3. List several characteristics of this period of middle adulthood.
4. What home adjustments do middle adults often experience?
5. What kind of fellowship is needed to measure up to New Testament standards?
6. How does the middle adult affect the church's ministry to children and youth?

Application Activities

1. Apply the five characteristics of this period to your own life.
2. Interview several middle adults regarding their experience with "mid-life crisis"? How were the individuals helped—or the cases resolved?
3. Discuss the social characteristics and needs of middle-aged adults as seen in immediate friends and relatives. Make a list of the main needs and suggest ways these needs can be met through your church program.

INDIAN SUMMER

LATER ADULTHOOD

Ages 65 and older

12

Older adulthood, while the sunset of life, is far more than a time of physical and mental decline. With long life, people will spend almost one-fourth of their lives as older adults. With the advances in medical science and more healthful living helping to add years to the life span, more adults are numbered in this age group now than ever before. This adult period may be thought of in terms of several periods: Young Old (65-74), Middle Old (75-84), Older Old (85-94), and Old Old (95 plus).

A Rewarding Age

Today, new interest is being shown in older adults. Studying the aging person and process has developed into a new science. The practice of geriatrics, which deals with the health of the aged, is expanding.

Old age does not come suddenly. Age is not entirely a matter of years. Some older adults may be younger in spirit at 70 than others at 50. These persons have a vital interest in life. Happy are those who plan for older adulthood and then learn to enjoy this time apart from demanding responsibilities.

According to Erikson, later maturity is characterized by "integrity vs. despair and disgust. Integrity is the acceptance on one's life cycle and the people who have been part of it. . . . The alternative is despair . . . and disgust with one's self, which is usually projected onto others." [1]

Fowler comments on this as follows: "Integrity is the fruit of a life that has found a basis for self-acceptance and for confirming one's life as worthwhile. Integrity seems to come with the considered feeling that one played the roles and met the challenges of each of the eras of the life cycle. It does not mean perfection; it does mean the absence of regrets. It does mean having found a way to make one's life count in caring for— and hopefully enhancing— the on-going flow of life. From the experiences one gathers, from the suffering and the gladness, one accrues the virture Erikson calls *wisdom*." [2]

Having no outside interests, living in the past, and not continuing to learn account for some of the reasons people fail to adjust to the problems of aging and living at this age. These problems could affect their Christian service as well. While some seem to drop out of church ministry when they become old, others find no reason to retire from serving God.

Later adulthood calls for simplifying life and enjoying those things of lasting value. "Though outwardly we are wasting away, yet inwardly we are being renewed day by day" (2 Cor. 4:16b).

Developmental Tasks

Havighurst lists the following developmental tasks for older adults:
> Adjusting to decreasing physical strength and health.
> Adjustment to retirement and reduced income.
> Adjusting to death of spouse.
> Establishing an explicit affiliation with one's age group.
> Meeting social and civic obligations.
> Establishing satisfactory physical living arrangements. [3]

Adding a note on the spiritual side— Happy are the adults who have walked with God in the adult years and continue to do so. For those who haven't, it isn't too late to start.

Physically — *Declining*

Inevitably, vital powers, bodily strength, and physical attractiveness decline. The beauty of old age, however, can come from within— from the soul and spirit.

Enjoy Limited Good Health

Senior adults usually enjoy good health in the early decade of this period— with limitations. The wisest older adults are those who learn to: take care of their health; live with necessary discomfort and pain; and listen to their doctor's advice to be realistic and temperate about physical activities.

Physical illness increases at this time, often causing confinement. Although not an automatic problem of aging, disease often becomes a factor in older adults' lives. Adults with chronic illnesses must adjust to disability and the social results of limited activity. Their body's metabolic energy, cell division, and repair rates decrease. Older adults are sometimes susceptible to broken bones as the bones become more brittle.

Some apparent evidences of physical decline are psychological. They may exaggerate disabilities allowing them to isolate themselves from their fellows and activities.

Intellectually — *Wise Counsel*

Accumulated knowledge, experienced judgment, and wise counsel make older adults valuable assets to the church, home, community, and nation. All benefit immeasurably from this stock of wisdom and maturity (Lev. 19:32; Prov. 16:31; 20:29; 23:22).

Have Modified Learning Performance

Older adults are able to learn but individual characteristics vary. Learning and intellectual performance is modified in a variety of ways: physiological condition, sensory decline, reaction time, lack of practice, outlook, status, social change, and motivation.

Mental and learning powers can be retained in varying degrees as long as the older adult lives. Attractive and worthwhile adult education can benefit the community and church.

Relive Past Experiences

Senior adults are retrospective, often reliving the past. They need to be encouraged to live in the present and anticipate the future. For Christians, this results in continuing discipleship and the blessed hope of seeing the Lord.

Senior adults should be aware of static patterns of living and inflexibility. They should look for the good and creative things in life.

Need to Keep Proper Mental Attitude

Older adults may be childish, suspicious, deceptive, and deeply depressed because of physical and mental deterioration. Developing new interests along with continued education and mental stimulation helps them keep a positive attitude. Older adults should feel they are useful, needed, able to help others, and that they can utilize past experience.

Emotionally — *Set Pattern*

Older adults can be either sweet and graceful or sour and bitter. The latter is usually caused by increasing emotional rigidity, repeated behavior, lack of effective adaptability, and less recovery from emotional experiences.

One study done on adults of this age level said that the emotional stature of older adults depends not only on present stresses and hardships but also upon their previous personality. It concluded that old persons are just what they were when they were young except more so. [4]

Some persons keep growing while others seem to give up emotionally. The friendly, thoughtful, and out-going become more so, the selfish become narrow and withdrawn. Resources of the Christian faith are needed to keep cheerful and optimistic, in spite of sin, sorrow, and suffering.

Need Self-Esteem

The study mentioned earlier went on to point out that a common emotional problem for aging adults is loss of self-esteem. They do not want to be set aside or to be treated as if they are no longer relevant but may not know how to avoid it and feel an inevitable loss of prestige among their family, friends, and associates.

They may employ certain defense mechanisms to cope with the situation, all of which seem real and logical to them. They may imagine themselves sick, turn to the past, refuse anything new, become self-assertive and domineering to compensate for inferiority and inadequacy.

For older adults who have always leaned heavily on others for moral support, financial dependency often can become a greater problem. The absence or death of this key person requires profound adjustments for these older adults which they may resist or have difficulty making. [5]

Adjust to Crises

Older adults must make a variety of other adjustments as they face several crisis periods associated with aging such as the death of a spouse or being confined to a home for the aged. Happy are those who can say, "The Lord is *my* shepherd," "The Lord is *my* helper," (Ps. 23:1; Heb. 13:6) in the midst of making adjustments to the crises of old age.

Socially — *Interests Narrow*

Senior citizens are less active in social functions but thrive on those programs organized for them. Because they have more leisure time most desire meaningful social lives. They enjoy talking and visiting with members of their own age group.

Enjoy Family Ties

The family circle is often the nucleus of their social life. They watch their children succeed and grandchildren grow with satisfaction and pride. Older adults who have good relations with their children and grandchildren have a headstart for pleasant experiences.

The ones who have no family or are rejected by their families can be extremely lonesome—as can adults who have lost their marriage partner.

Desire Social Relationships

Older adults desire social relationships but are frustrated by inner rigidity and self-isolation, geographical separation, other communication barriers, and many lack adequate finances.

Approval by peers and leaders motivates older adults and disapproval discourages them. Educational and recreational endeavors help. Group travel is also popular. They enjoy release from living by the clock but want to be busy.

In order to replace social relationships previously developed in their vocations, aging adults should be encouraged to continue activities in organized groups such as church, social groups, retirement clubs, civic and political organizations.

Spiritually — *Testing Time*

"Life's testing time" can be the height of spiritual development, evidencing rich Christian character, or it may lack interest in spiritual things entirely. Older adults may become more Christ-like with each year, or may become hardened to the gospel and the claims of Christ.

The fact that many older adults do not personally trust and love the Lord Jesus Christ makes evangelism a continuing priority.

Older adults generally have much time for contemplation and may live with regrets or despise former busyness. They need not regret the past. They, too, as Paul, can press on to new ventures, "Forgetting what is behind, and straining toward what is ahead" (Phil. 3:13b).

Implications for Ministry

Ministry to older adults can help them see their later years as golden years for Christian service and growth. Programming should be set up to meet these basic needs—fellowship with other Christians, Bible study, worship, meditation, prayer, witness, and service.

An active church welcomes the challenge of ministering to senior citizens. Charles Gresham suggests the following principles:

Assess the needs of your church and community.

Provide leadership.

Let older people help plan their own programs.

Use group-work principles.

Remember that older people need fun too.

Do not overlook the individual person. [6]

Older adult ministries also need to provide for shut-ins, bringing them the benefits of Bible study, worship, and fellowship. Home visitation is the primary method employed, and specific materials for reading and study are provided. Many times older adults themselves can help carry on this ministry.

Some type of club or center should be provided either by the community or church. Older adults should not be isolated to their own programs only, but should be made to feel a vital part of the entire church program, especially fellowship times, special events, and activities. They can have a healthy and wholesome influence on the church's children and youth and they on older adults. The church can benefit from older adults' surplus of time for assisting with leadership roles, visitation, teaching, and counseling (Ps. 71:18; Titus 2:1-5). Even those who are shut in can have a vital prayer and letter-writing ministry, or work at folding, stuffing envelopes, or cutting out handwork for children's programs. Those who are more young at heart and physically able can tend to groundskeeping chores or assist in weekday club work, vacation Bible school, or camp programs.

Summary

Later adulthood can be the most rewarding of life. It is the age of wise counsel and continued learning. Social interests often narrow—though not always by choice. Increasing emotional rigidity is often evidenced, yet many continue to mature emotionally. Many adjustments need to be made to live out these years successfully. It's not too late to reach the unsaved—but time is running out. It's a time for spiritual growth and continued service for these important members of the church.

Notes

1. Erik H. Erikson, *Identity and the Life Cycle* (New York: International Universities Press, 1959), pp. 95-99.
2 James W. Fowler, *Becoming Adult, Becoming Christian, Adult Development and Christian Faith* (San Francisco: Harper and Row Publishers, 1984), p. 26.
3. R. J. Havighurst, *Human Development and Education* (New York: David McKay Co., 1953), pp. 257-67.
4. *The Age Group Objectives of Christian Education*, The Boards of Parish Education for four Lutheran churches (Philadelphia: W. Kent Gilbert, 1958), p. 93.
5. *The Age Group Objectives of Christian Education*, pp. 93-96
6. Charles Gresham, *Adult Department* (Cincinnati: Standard Publishing, 1966), p. 38.

Discussion Questions

1. How do the older adults you know show Havighurst's signs of development?
2. How can senior adults be inspired to face today's challenges rather than just continuing to review yesterday's successes?
3. Why is evangelism still important in ministering to this age level?
4. Briefly charactize the older adult physically.
5. What are the key factors in considering the social characteristics and needs of older adults?
6. What are some of the challenges involved in ministering to older adults' spiritual needs?

Application Activities

1. Make a list of ways younger people can bring joy to older adults?
2. Think about what you can do now to try to become the person you wish to be in old age?
3. Discuss ways of effectively utilizing the time and talents of older adults in the church's ministry. Prepare a definite list which could be submitted to a church board for implementation.
4. Interview a variety of senior adults to find out their distinctive charactertistics and needs. Compare their feelings about life—past, present, and future.

RESOURCES FOR ENRICHMENT

Children

Barbour, Mary A. *You Can Teach 2's and 3's.* Wheaton, IL: Scripture Press/Victor Books, 1974.

Beechick, Ruth. *Teaching Juniors.* Denver: Accent Books, 1981.

_____. *Teaching Kindergartners.* Denver: Accent Books, 1980.

_____. *Teaching Preschoolers.* Denver: Accent Books, 1979.

Bolton, Barbara J. and Smith, Charles T. *Creative Bible Learning for Children.* Ventura, CA: Gospel Light/Regal Books, 1977.

Clark, Robert E. *Teaching Preschoolers with Confidence.* Wheaton, IL: Evangelical Training Assn., 1983.

Dobson, James. *Dare to Discipline.* Wheaton, IL: Tyndale House, 1970.

Gangel, Elizabeth and McDaniel, Elsiebeth. *You Can Reach Families Through Their Babies.* Wheaton, IL: Victor Books, 1976.

Gibson, Joyce and Hance, Eleanor. *You Can Teach Juniors and Middlers.* Wheaton, IL: Scripture Press, 1981.

Haystead, Wesley. *Teaching Your Child About God.* Ventura, CA: Gospel Light/Regal Books, 1978.

How To Do Bible Learning Activities: Early Childhood. Ventura, CA: Gospel Light/Regal Books, 1982.

How To Do Bible Learning Activities: Grades 1-6. 2 vols. Ventura, CA: Gospel Light/Regal Books, 1984.

Jenkins, David, *Teaching Children with Confidence.* Wheaton, IL: Evangelical Training Assn., 1983.

LeBar, Mary, and Riley, Betty. *You Can Teach 4's and 5's.* Wheaton, IL: Scripture Press/Victor Books, 1981.

McDaniel, Elsiebeth. *You Can Teach Primaries.* Wheaton, IL: Scripture Press, 1981.

Meier, Paul D. *Christian Child-Rearing and Personality Development.* Grand Rapids: Baker Book House, 1977.

Price, B. Max. *Understanding Today's Children.* Nashville: Convention Press, 1982.

Schimmels, Cliff. *The First Three Years of School: A Survivor's Guide.* Old Tappan, NJ: Fleming H. Revell, 1985.

Soderholm, Marjorie. *Explaining Salvation to a Child.* Minneapolis: Free Church Publications, 1979.

Strickland, Jenell, comp. *How to Guide Preschoolers.* Nashville: Convention Press, 1982.

Waldrop, C. Sybil. *Guiding Your Child Toward God.* Nashville: Broadman Press, 1985.

_____. *Understanding Today's Preschoolers.* Nashville: Convention Press, 1982.

Wand, Zadabeth. *Bible Teaching for Preschoolers.* Nashville: Convention Press, 1984.

Adolescence

Aleshire, O. Daniel. *Understanding Today's Youth.* Nashville: Convention Press, 1982.

Benson, Warren S. and Senter, Mark. *The Complete Book of Youth Ministry.* Chicago: Moody Press, 1988.

Borthwick, Paul. *Organizing Your Youth Ministry.* Grand Rapids: Zondervan Publishing, 1988.

Bynum, Bill. *Teaching Youth with Confidence.* Wheaton, IL: Evangelical Training Assn., 1983.

Cagle, Bob. *Youth Ministry Camping.* Loveland, CO: Group Books, 1989.

Dausey, Gary, ed. *The Youth Leader's Source Book.* Grand Rapids: Zondervan Publishing, 1983.

Dobson, James. *Preparing for Adolescence.* Santa Ana, CA: Vision House Publishers, 1980.

Johnson, Lin. *Teaching Junior Highers.* Denver: Accent Books, 1986.

Kesler, Jay. *Parents and Teenagers.* Wheaton, IL: Victor Books, 1984.

Narramore, Bruce. *Adolescence Is Not An Illness.* Old Tappan, NJ: Fleming H. Revell, 1980.

Nordtvedt, Matilda and Steinkuehler, Pearl. *Ideas for Jr. High Leaders.* Chicago: Moody Press, 1983.

Olson, G. Keith. *Counseling Teenagers.* Loveland, CO: Group Books, 1984.

Power Pak Series. *How To Books for Youth Leaders, Jr. High/Sr. High.* Wheaton, IL: Victor Books.

Richards, Lawrence O. *The "Answers for Youth" Series.* Grand Rapids: Zondervan Publishing, 1980.

Schimmels, Cliff. *When Junior Highs Invade Your Home.* Old Tappan, NJ: Fleming H. Revell Co., 1984.

Strommen, Merton P. and Strommen, Irene A. *Five Cries of Parents.* San Francisco: Harper and Row Publishers, 1985.

Zuck, Roy B. and Benson, Warren S. *Youth Education in the Church.* Chicago: Moody Press, 1978.

Adulthood

Coleman, Lucien E. *Understanding Today's Adults.* Nashville: Convention Press, 1982.

Collins, Gary. *Toward a Growing Marriage.* Chicago: Moody Press, 1979.

Conway, James. *Men in Mid-Life Crisis.* Elgin, IL: David C. Cook Publishing Co., 1978.

DATE DUE

Cooper, Polly. *How to Guide Adults.* Nashville:

Jacobsen, Henry. *You Can Teach Adults.* Wh
    1981.

LeFeber, Larry. *Building a Young Adult Mini*
    Press, 1980.

Loth, Paul E. *Teaching Adults With Conf*
    Training Assn., 1984.

Narramore, Clyde and Ruth. *Hov*
    dale House, 1975.

Peterson, Gilbert A. *The Chris*
    Press, 1987.

Sell, Charles M. *Transition.* Chicago: M

Towns, Elmer. *The Single Adult and the Church.*
    1967.

Wood, Britton. *Single Adults Want to be the Church Too.* N
    tion Press, 1982.

Zuck, Roy B. and Getz, Gene A., eds. *Adult Education in the*
    Chicago: Moody Press, 1970.

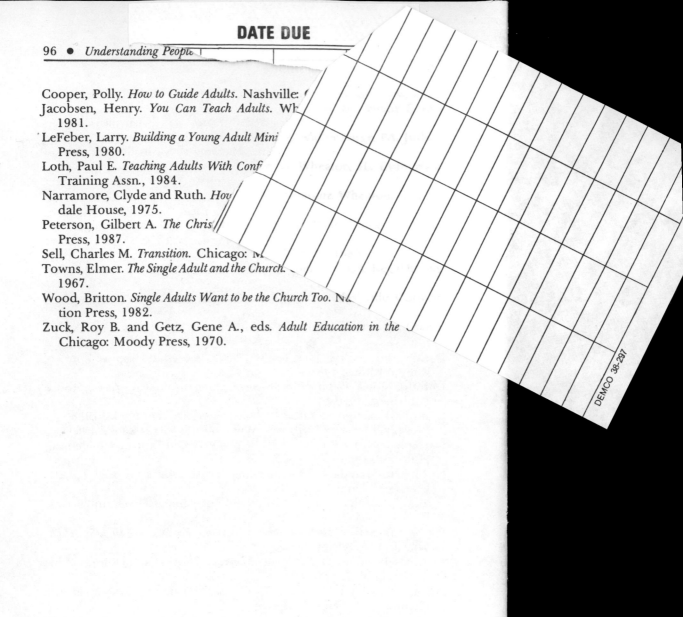

DEMCO 38-297